# BOTTOMS UP

## A Walking Guide to
## Hull Pubs

## Howard B Fuller

Highgate Publications (Beverley) Ltd
1993

British Library Cataloguing in Publication Data
Fuller, Howard Brant
  Bottoms Up: Walking Guide to Hull Pubs
  I. Title
  647.9542837

  ISBN 0-948929-73-1

ISBN 0 948929 73 1

Published by
Highgate Publications (Beverley) Ltd.
24 Wylies Road, Beverley, HU17 7AP
Telephone (0482) 866826

Produced by
B. A. Print
4 Newbegin, Lairgate, Beverley, HU17 8EG
Telephone (0482) 886017

*Cover Pictures: Jonathan White*

# CONTENTS

*Page*

# FOREWORD

'It's never dull in Hull' is a phrase fast becoming part of our City's unofficial phrase book — and Howard Fuller is one reason why it's in such popular usage.

Howard's love of local history is infectious. This, coupled with his long experience in the licensed trade, has enabled him to offer us *Bottoms Up* — a unique insight into the City of Hull's distinctive history.

As a relative newcomer to Hull, I was honoured to be a 'guinea pig' for the now infamous 'Howard's Way' tours of the City centre pubs. *Bottoms Up* makes a night out to the pub a truly educational and thoroughly entertaining experience.

You now have the opportunity to sample the City's beers whilst discovering secret rooms, smugglers' tunnels, arsenals and centres of commerce. Through pub names, locations and information about the past use of the buildings Howard has pieced together a story of Hull's development, the people who have played an important role in the City, and its position nationally.

*Bottoms Up* is overflowing with over 500 years of the history of Hull. If it can bring half the pleasure to you that Howard Fuller's tours have to many of his friends, then I guarantee you will not be disappointed.

Tom Watson
President
Hull University Students Union (1992-3)

# INTRODUCTION

The history of Hull is rich and fascinating, but its importance and the significant role the town and its people have played on the national stage have long been understated. Hull's easy access to the Humber estuary has played a major part in its development as a long established port, bringing great prosperity to the town. By 1964 its docks were handling cargoes of some 10 million tons annually and housed what was considered to be the world's largest fishing fleet. Its status as one of Britain's principal ports had been maintained ever since Edward I recognised the importance in 1293 of the former trading settlements known as Wyke and Myton-on-Hull and renamed them King's Town-on-Hull, now, of course, abbreviated to Kingston upon Hull.

With this prosperity came people, and what better reward for their labours after a hard day's work than a mug of ale. Indeed, at one time part of a worker's wages was often paid in beer. The expression, *'I'll take him down a peg or two'*, relates directly to this practice. An old drinking vessel known as a Peg O'Wassail was of leather construction made into the shape of a horn, with four pegs placed in its sides, dividing the horn into four equal drinkable sections. If the employer was dissatisfied with your work, he would remove a peg... those were the days!

Hull, it seems, had a reputation for serving up the finest. Amongst many recorded compliments is one from the naturalist, Clayton Edward Ray, who wrote in 1661, *'Hull is noted for good ale'*, and Andrew Marvell, MP for Hull and celebrated poet, wrote from his London home, in 1658, acknowledging a present of a *'cask of prime ale from Hull'*.

The town had its fair share of local brewers providing this delightful mixture of malt, hops, sugar, yeast and water to a vast array of drinking outlets. Sadly, the passing of time has witnessed a reduction in the number of these establishments. The ceasing of whaling, long and bitter dockland disputes and the decline of Hull's once-proud fishing industry, prompted by Britain's entry into the Common Market (1972) and the subsequent Icelandic Cod Wars, have all contributed to the town's diminished importance as an international port.

Of late, the waterfronts are enjoying a renaissance, with the development of the Marina, opened by HM the Queen in 1987, and the recently opened Princes Quay shopping complex. St Andrew's Dock has become the setting of a modern leisure and business park and new prestige housing developments throughout the Old Town and docklands are in abundance, all playing their part in Hull's revival and survival as a truly great city. This revival is witnessing the birth of new public houses and rebirth of others, and so helping to ensure a wide and diverse selection of watering-holes for today's discerning drinker.

We are nonetheless fortunate in inheriting a legacy of some wonderful public houses where one can enjoy this most pleasurable of pastimes, many not only providing good ale but also rich in history. Their histories are inextricably linked with Hull's past, which their names and locations reflect and celebrate. There is no better place to experience the continuity between past and present than Hull's city centre and Old Town. To help you along your way I have put together this 'beerlet' which takes the form of three pub tours designed to enable you to drink in as much history as you do ale.

I have always subscribed to Oscar Wilde's view that... *'work is the curse of the drinking classes'*, and having tried and tested, or should it be tasted (I forget which), these routes, I am even more convinced.

Cheers

This book is dedicated to
**Dinah, Victoria, Charlotte and Madelaine**
**for their patience and understanding during its compilation.**

# ACKNOWLEDGEMENTS

It has given me immense personal pleasure to research this guide but these efforts would not have been possible without the help I have received from a whole host of people. This is especially true of all the ladies of Hull's Local Studies Library without whose assistance I would not have dared put pen to paper. To them I say a special thank you. I would also like to thank Tom Watson and all the members of the General Purposes Committee (1992-3) Hull University Students Union for giving me the inspiration to research this book. Particular mention must be given to Sharon Hart (first draft) and Joanne Young (final script) for their excellent typing services, crossing my t's and dotting my i's, and to Adam Stewart and Jonathon White, my intrepid cameramen. I am also grateful for the help I have received from M J Astbury, Clerk to the Licensing Justices, Arthur Credland, Keeper of Maritime History, Hull City Museums and Art Galleries, Trinity House, Hull, Sarah Elsom, Curator, Bass Museum (Staffordshire), and the staff of Hull's Central Reference Library, the Local History Unit, Park Street and the Kingston upon Hull Record Office. I am indebted to all the licensees, staff and customers involved in this publication for sparing their valuable time. I have almost exclusively taken street descriptions from my editor, John Markham's excellent book *Streets of Hull*, a 'read' I would heartily recommend to everyone.

Sources I have consulted include the following:

Allison, K J (ed)     *The Victoria History of the County of York, East Riding, Vol. 1*

Barnard, Robert     *Barley Mash and Yeast*

Bickford (Dr), J A R     *The Medical Profession in Hull (1400-1900)*

Croft-Cooke, Rupert     *Buffalo Bill*

Evans, Jeff (ed)     *Good Beer Guide*

Hall, Ivan and
Elizabeth     *Georgian Hull*

Henrey, Blanche     *No Ordinary Gardener*

Fowler, Mary     *Holderness Road*

Markham, John     *Colourful Characters*

Markham, John     *Streets of Hull*

| | |
|---|---|
| Parker, Brian | *The Symbols of Sovereignty* |
| Pepper, Barrie | *A Haunt of Rare Souls* |
| Sheppard, Thomas | *Evolution of the Drama in Hull* |
| Wilson-Smith, J | *Hull and Holderness* |
| Wrigglesworth, Edmund | *Brown's Illustrated Guide to Hull* |

Other sources consulted in Hull Central Library include: *Modern Hull 1893* (scrapbook), *Ye Olde White Harte Companie 1883*, T. Sheppard Pamphlets, Collected cuttings of A. E. Trout, Hull directories, *Hull Daily Mail*, *Hull Times*, *Hull Arrow*, *Eastern Morning News*, *Sunday Times*, *Pub Mirror*.

# BREWS LISTED IN THIS GUIDE

| *Product* | *Brewer* | *ABV* |
|---|---|---|
| **BITTER** | | |
| Bass | Bass | 4.4 |
| Bass Best Scotch | Bass | 3.6 |
| Bass Light | Bass | 3.3 |
| Bateman Salem Porter | G Bateman (Skegness) | 5.0 |
| Bateman XXXB | G Bateman (Skegness) | 5.0 |
| Blacksheep Special | Blacksheep (Masham) | 4.4 |
| Boddingtons | Whitbread | 3.8 |
| Butter Knowle Conciliation | Butter Knowle | 4.2 |
| Chainmaker Stonehenge | Pitfield's (Stourbridge) | 3.6 |
| Clark's Festival | H B Clark & Co | 4.2 |
| Directors | Courage | 4.8 |
| Everards Tiger | Everards (Narborough) | 4.2 |
| Exhibition | Scottish & Newcastle | 4.3 |
| Flowers Original | Whitbread | 4.5 |
| Hambleton Porter | Hambleton (Thirsk) | 3.7 |
| Hull Brewery | Hull Brewery Co | 3.6 |
| John Smith's | Courage | 3.8 |
| King Billy Bitter | New Inn (Cropton) | 3.8 |
| Mansfield | Mansfield | 3.9 |
| Malton Double Chance | Malton Brewery Co | 4.0 |
| Marston's Pedigree | Marston, Thompson & Evershed | 4.5 |
| McEwan's Export | Scottish & Newcastle | 4.5 |
| Mitchell's ESB | Mitchell's (Lancaster) | 5.2 |
| Museum Strong | Samuel Smith's | 5.0 |
| Old Baily | Mansfield | 4.8 |
| Old Brewery | Samuel Smith's | 3.8 |
| Old Mill | Old Mill (Snaith) | 3.7 |
| Old Peculier | Scottish & Newcastle (Theakston) | 5.6 |
| Riding | Mansfield | 3.6 |
| Rooster Yankee | Roosters (Harrogate) | 4.3 |

| Product | Brewer | ABV |
|---|---|---|
| Samson | Vaux | 4.1 |
| Stones | Bass | 4.1 |
| Tetley | Allied Breweries (Tetley) | 3.6 |
| The Governor | Hull Brewery | 4.8 |
| Theakston Best | Scottish & Newcastle (Theakston) | 3.8 |
| Theakston XB | Scottish & Newcastle (Theakston) | 4.5 |
| Thorne Best | Vaux (S. H. Ward) | 3.9 |
| Timothy Taylor's Landlord | Timothy Taylor & Co | 4.3 |
| Vaux Pale Ale | Vaux | 3.0 |
| Wadworth's 6X | Wadworth & Co | 4.3 |
| Wards Sheffield Best | Vaux (S H Ward) | 4.0 |
| Webster's | Courage | 3.8 |
| Worthington Best | Bass | 3.8 |
| Younger's IPA | Scottish & Newcastle | 4.5 |
| Younger's N° 3 | Scottish & Newcastle | 4.5 |

LAGER

| | | |
|---|---|---|
| Ayingerbräu* | Ayingerbräu (Bavaria) | 4.5 |
| Ayingerbräu D Pils* | Ayingerbräu (Bavaria) | 5.9 |
| Beck's | Beck's (Bremen) | 5.0 |
| Carling Black Label | Bass | 4.1 |
| Carlsberg Export* | Carlsberg (Copenhagen) | 4.7 |
| Carlton LA | Courage | 0.9 |
| Castlemaine XXXX* | Castlemaine Perkins (Australia) | 3.9 |
| Coors Extra Gold* | Coors Brewing Co (USA) | 5.0 |
| Foster's* | Carlton United Brewers (Australia) | 3.6 |
| Grolsch | Grolsch (Holland) | 5.0 |
| Heineken* | Heineken (Holland) | 3.4 |
| Kaliber | Arthur Guinness | 0.05 |
| Kronenbourg* | Kronenbourg (Strasbourg) | 5.0 |
| Labatt's* | Labatt's (Canada) | 5.0 |
| Löwenbräu* | Löwenbräu AG (Munich) | 5.0 |
| Marksman | Mansfield | 4.1 |
| McEwan's | Scottish & Newcastle | 4.1 |
| Miller Pilsner* | Miller Brewing Co (USA) | 4.2 |
| Red Stripe* | Desnoes Geddes (Jamaica) | 4.8 |
| Skol | Allied Breweries | 3.8 |
| Stella Artois* | Stella Artois (Belgium) | 5.1 |
| Tennent's Extra | Bass (Tennent's Caledonian) | 5.0 |
| Tennent's LA | Bass (Tennent's Caledonian) | 1.0 |
| Tennent's Pilsner | Bass (Tennent's Caledonian) | 3.8 |

| Product | Brewer | ABV |
|---|---|---|
| **CIDER** | | |
| Autumn Gold | Taunton Cider Co | 5.0 |
| Copperhead | Coates Gaymer's | 4.5 |
| Dry Blackthorn | Taunton Cider Co | 5.0 |
| Olde English | Coates Gaymer's | 4.5 |
| Sam Smith's Reserve | Samuel Smith's | 5.0 |
| Scrumpy Jack | Symonds Cider Co | 6.0 |
| Strongbow | H P Bulmer | 4.5 |
| Weston Old Rosie | Weston's of Hereford | 7.3 |
| Woodpecker | H P Bulmer | 4.0 |
| | | |
| **MILD** | | |
| Bass | Bass | 3.3 |
| Chestnut | Courage (John Smith's) | 3.0 |
| Darley's | Vaux (Wards) | 3.2 |
| Hull Brewery | Hull Brewery | 3.2 |
| Riding | Mansfield | 3.5 |
| Sam Smith's Dark | Samuel Smith's | 3.0 |
| Tetley | Allied Breweries (Tetley) | 3.2 |
| Thorne Dark | Vaux | 3.4 |
| Wilson's Original | Courage | 3.0 |
| | | |
| **OTHER** | | |
| Beamish | Beamish & Crawford | 4.0 |
| Guinness | Arthur Guinness | 4.1 |
| Murphy's* | Murphy's of Cork | 4.0 |
| Sam Smith's Extra Stout | Samuel Smith's | 4.1 |
| Selby Old Tom | Selby Brewery (Middlebrough) | 6.5 |

* Brewed under licence in the UK

The public houses in this guide were visited between November 1992 and July 1993 and every effort has been made to ensure that information is as accurate and up-to-date as possible.

**Abbreviations used in this guide:**
ABV — Alcohol by Volume
cc — Cask Conditioned
(g) — Guest Beer
CAMRA — Campaign for Real Ale
CALM — Campaign against Loud Music

# The Old Town

(Map not to scale)

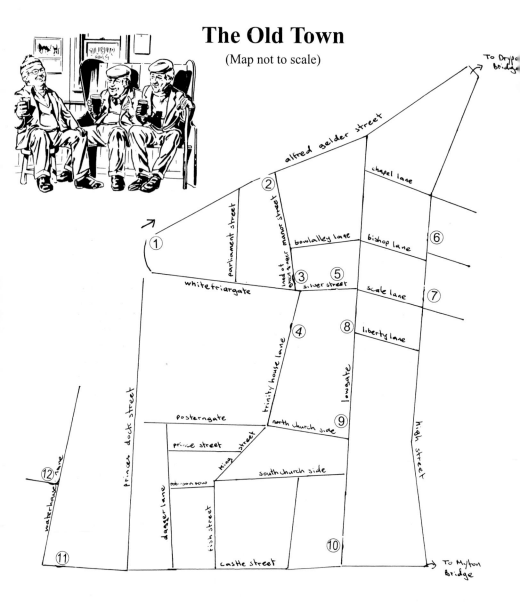

To Drypo Bridge

alfred gelder street

chapel lane

② parliament street

indot open anor street

bowlalley lane

bishop lane

⑥

① whitefriargate

③ silver street ⑤

scale lane

⑦

④ trinity house lane

⑧ liberty lane

lowgate

princes dock street

posterngate

prince street

king street

north church side ⑨

high street

⑫ waterhouse lane

dagger lane

robinson row

fish street

south church side

castle street

⑪

⑩

To Myton Bridge

1. The Empress Hotel  2. Burlington Tavern  3. The George Hotel  4. The Bonny Boat
5. Ye Olde White Harte  6. The Sailmakers Arms  7. Ye Olde Black Boy
8. Ye Olde Blue Bell  9. Ye Olde Corn Exchange  10. King Wiliam  11. Earl de Grey
12. The Royal William

# HOWARD'S WAY (Part One) — THE OLD TOWN

| | | |
|---|---|---|
| The Empress Hotel | Alfred Gelder Street | Tel: 26839 |
| Burlington Tavern | Manor Street | Tel: 223928 |
| The George Hotel | Land of Green Ginger | Tel: 226373 |
| The Bonny Boat | Trinity House Lane | Tel: 224961 |
| Ye Olde White Harte | Silver Street | Tel: 26363 |
| The Sailmakers Arms | Chandlers Court | Tel: 227437 |
| Ye Olde Black Boy | High Street | Tel: 26516 |
| Ye Olde Blue Bell | Market Place | Tel: 24382 |
| Ye Olde Corn Exchange | North Church Side | Tel: 26366 |
| King William | Market Place | Tel: 23997 |
| Earl de Grey | Castle Street | Tel: 24989 |
| The Royal William | Waterhouse Lane | Tel: 215881 |

**THE EMPRESS HOTEL** — COURAGE

Designed by J Hirst, the renowned architect who also designed Hull's City Hall, this tall, impressive four-storeyed house is one of Hull's most distinctive public houses. The original Empress which stood on this spot was demolished in 1903 during the laying out of Alfred Gelder Street.

It was called the Dock Tavern c.1790 before being re-named the Old Dock Tavern by 1803. Hull's first dock was opened in 1778 and was situated where Queen's Gardens is now. It was then simply known as 'The Dock'. It is usually stated that the term 'Old Dock' came into use when the 'New Dock' (Humber Dock) was opened in 1809, but the name of this inn shows that it was used earlier. After Queen Victoria's visit to Hull in 1854 it was named in her honour, Queen's Dock. A former licensee, a German named Westeroff, applied to the local licensing magistrates to change the pub's name when Queen Victoria became Empress of India (1876). This was duly granted but only on the proviso that, in due deference to the Queen, it did not trade on a Sunday; there are

1

*The Empress Hotel*
Adam Stewart

no such rest-rictions these days. Another li-censee, William Whileyman, was an intelligence of-ficer during the First World War.

Construction of Alfred Gelder Street began in 1901 and it was named in honour of Alfred Gelder (1855-1941). He was a prominent architect and politician of his day, being Mayor of Hull a record five times in succession (1898-1903). He was responsible for much of today's layout of the City centre and heavily involved in the filling in of the former Queen's Dock and creation of Queen's Gardens. The offices of Kitchen and Gelder, the firm in which he practised, are still with us today and are situated within one of Hull's most historic buildings, Maister House, 160 High Street, now the property of the National Trust.

Bitter:    John Smith's<sup>cc</sup>
Lager:    Miller Pilsner, Foster's, Kronenbourg, Kaliber
Cider:    Woodpecker, Strongbow
Other:    Chestnut Mild, Guinness
Bar meals and sandwiches are available Monday — Thursday all day. Friday and Saturday, 11.00am — 3.00pm.
Jukebox

## BURLINGTON TAVERN — BASS

This house was originally established as the Bridlington Tavern c.1770 but by 1826 had become the Burlington. The old town of Bridlington, a fishing port on the east coast, was originally called Burlington: hence the name.

The portrait on the sign displayed at the front of the pub is of Richard Boyle, 3rd Earl of Burlington, and is not, as stated, George Augustus Cavendish, 1st Earl of Burlington. Richard Boyle, the 3rd Earl (1695-1753), is perhaps the most famous member of this landed family, being dubbed 'the architect earl'. He introduced Palladian architecture to Britain and amongst his more notable achievements were the designs of Chiswick House in London, the York Assembly Rooms and the dormitory of Westminster School. It is also thought that he was involved in the rebuilding of one of Hull's finest homes, Maister House, situated in High Street, which was seriously damaged by a fire on the night of 12-13 April 1743. A letter sent to its owner Henry Maister from his brother Nathaniel, records:

*'Musgrave says my Lord Burlington don't approve of the cornice you have pitched upon. He says it must be a plain one and has promised upon Musgrave's reminding him when he gets to town to send a draught of one that will be suitable.'*

*Burlington Tavern*                                    *Adam Stewart*

3

Richard Boyle had vast estates at Londesborough near Market Weighton and very strong East Yorkshire connections. His gardener, Thomas Knowlton, owned a tract of land in Hull close to the site of the present Mason Street. He was one of the most outstanding horticulturists of his time, his skill and cultivation of exotic plants was widely recognised and his advice and 'green fingers' much sought after. One of the property owners he advised was William Constable of Burton Constable Hall, and he corresponded with most of the great gardeners of his day. Several species of plants are named after him.

To return to George Cavendish, mentioned earlier, Debretts of London inform me that the title of 1st Earl of Burlington was a 'second creation' of the title given to Cavendish in 1831. Confused? So am I! He was related to the Dukes of Devonshire, as the architect Richard Boyle's daughter, Charlotte, had married into the family: hence the connection. Incidentally, Thomas Knowlton was employed successively by the 3rd, 4th and 5th Dukes of Devonshire following the 3rd Earl of Burlington's death.

For a short time during the 1840s this pub was known as the Wellington, and as it stands opposite Hull's Law Courts it enjoys the nicknames of the 'Witnesses' and 'Convict Arms'. Pictures of High Court Judges abound in this house as do some interesting transcripts of famous court battles by courtesy of the *London Illustrated News*. It is rare that one sees a member of the legal fraternity in this establishment, not even for a brief visit (no pun intended) . . . I wonder why?

Manor Street refers to the medieval manor house once occupied by the de la Poles, wealthy Hull merchants, which stood where the Post Office was later built.

Bitter: Bass[cc], Stones[cc]
Lager: Carling Black Label, Tennent's Pilsner, Beck's
Cider: Dry Blackthorn, Autumn Gold
Other: Bass Mild[cc], Guinness
Bar meals and sandwiches are available Monday — Saturday, 12.00 noon — 2.00pm
Jukebox, Darts

## THE GEORGE HOTEL — BASS

Formerly an Elizabethan mansion, The George is probably Hull's most continuously licensed public house. Evidence suggests that it was once the home of John Oversale, Sheriff of Hull in 1546 and Mayor in 1550. By 1680 it is reputed to have been trading as Ye White Frere Hostel, although by this time the original house had been replaced. The last monarch of the Stuart line, Queen Anne, was on the throne during this

*The George Hotel* *Adam Stewart*

period and it seems probable that shortly after her marriage to her popular consort, Prince George of Denmark, in 1683, the event was commemorated by christening this hostelry The George. This house was also known as The George Hotel Vaults in the early 1850s. You will notice a portrait of King George IV currently displayed as the pub's sign. As his reign was 1820-1830, long after the pub's name came into existence, I would venture to suggest that this is one part of his former kingdom where he has no business to be.

Another theory is that The George took its name from the Arms of St George, patron saint of the Company and Guild of Hull Merchants, incorporated in 1524 by Henry VIII, which traded near the site.

A popular former coaching inn, it is also reputed to have the smallest window in Hull and probably the smallest pub window in the UK (can you spot it?). In fact, this was used as a bootboy's spyhole when a boot house was incorporated into yet another re-build of the hotel which took place in the early 1860s. The contract for this work was awarded to Charles Hutchinson, a builder, from the appropriately named nearby George Yard.

By the turn of the century it was a thriving emporium of commerce, with restaurants, coffee and billiard rooms, a fine auction room and much of the first floor devoted to traders' stockrooms, together with 40 letting bedrooms on the top floor.

We almost lost this historic hostelry in 1934 when British Home Stores bought The George to develop its store (now Superdrug). A part of the inn which fronted Whitefriargate at that time has been demolished, but the George as we know it today survives. Much of its traditional character is retained today, with shuttered windows, panelled walls and bare boarded floors and it plays host to many of Hull's legal and professional fraternity.

The Land of Green Ginger is one of England's most unusual street names. Stories abound as to how it became so called. I find G J Monson-Fitzjohn's account the most credible of all. He was a Fellow of the Royal Historical Society and he explains that in the 1500s this plot of land was known as Old Beverley Street. A farmer-come-merchant from Lincolnshire, John Monson, built himself a palatial home here which bordered the grounds of Suffolk Palace, the home of the influential de la Poles, where Henry VIII stayed in 1540. King Hal was known to be partial to a table delicacy called green ginger which, steeped in wine, honey, lemon juice and flavoured with cloves, he found irresistible. Monson was known to have imported and attempted to cultivate this plant at the family home in South Kelsey and there is good reason to suppose that he did the same here in order to gain favour with the King, for shortly afterwards Old Beverley Street was known as Gingerland.

Other theories put forward which must be treated with the greatest suspicion include a story that a Dutch family called Lindegroen settled here, a junior member of which would be known in Dutch as 'Lindegroen jonger', a corruption of which led to Land of Green Ginger. Another theory, that the street is named after a boat-builder, Moses Greenhinger, has been debunked: he never existed.

Bitter:   Bass[cc], Tetley[cc], Stones
Lager:   Carling Black Label, Tennent's Pilsner, Tennent's LA
Cider:   Strongbow, Woodpecker
Other:   Bass Mild[cc], Guinness, Beamish
Bar meals and sandwiches are available Monday — Saturday, 12.00 noon — 2.30pm. The George also houses an excellent restaurant on its first floor. Monday — Friday, luncheon, 12.00 noon — 2.00pm; Monday — Saturday, evening, 7.00pm — 10.30pm
CAMRA recommended 1993

## THE BONNY BOAT — MANSFIELD

This house was called the Bank Hotel c.1790, reputedly reflecting the banking and commercial institutions then being established in the Old Town.

According to oral tradition its name was changed to The Bonny Boat

to attract seamen. In 1613, Captain Andrew Barker picked up an Eskimo and his kayak off the coast of Greenland and brought them back to England. The Eskimo apparently died three days later of self-imposed starvation. The kayak, along with the Eskimo's clothing, was put on public display in Trinity House, Hull, where they remain today. In 1697 a famous traveller of her day, Celia Fiennes, visited Trinity House and, later wrote,

*'In the town there is an hospitall thats called the Trinity House, for Seamens widdows, 30 is their compliment their allowance 16 pence per weeke and fewell, they have a little Chapple to it for prayers: over this building is a large roome for cordage and sailes, where they make them and keep their stores: in the middle of this roome there hangs a Canooe to the roofe of the roome, just bigg enough for one man to sit in, and the Effigie of a Man that was taken with it, all his Cloths Cap and a large Bag behind him where in his fish and provision were, these were all made of the skin of fishes and were the same which he wore when taken, for forme*

*of his face is only added and just resemble the Wildman that they took, for so the Inscription calls him or the Bonny Boatesman: he was taken by Captain Baker and there are his oars and spear that was with him: he would not speake any language or word to them that took him nor would he eate, so in a few dayes died.'*

During the late 1800s former landlord, Tom Jackson, closed this house because the brewery at that time refused to provide any toilet facilities for ladies. Needless to say, alterations were hastily made to accommodate this important facility. Another former landlord Armourer Sergeant Major Cox, who died in 1928, was reputed to be the oldest Regimental Sergeant Major in the British Army, serving mainly in India.

As you would expect 'we're all at sea' when entering this cosy one-bar pub, with plenty of captains' wheels and seamen's knick-knacks in evidence. Some fine green glazed tile-work on its frontage displays the motifs of what appear to be two lovers enjoying a pleasant day's sailing. The pub stands opposite Trinity House, which was originally founded as a religious guild in 1369, becoming a seamen's guild in 1456. The present building was erected in 1753 and occupies the site of the former Carmelite Friary home of the White Friars, dissolved by Henry VIII in 1539.

Today, Hull's Trinity House's purpose is mainly a charitable one, providing practical help to its members. It has 56 rest homes situated on Anlaby Road and awards *ex gratia* pension payments to needy retired seamen. Trinity House subscribes to Hull's Navigation School, now a voluntary aided school funded by Humberside County Council. The school, located on Princes Dock Side, was founded in 1787, and its pupils, bedecked in their fine uniforms, can often be seen strolling along the streets of the Old Town. Hitherto a male-only domain, it has accepted its first female student, Lisa Hannan, in its new year's intake of 1993.

Bitter:   Riding<sup>cc</sup>, Mansfield
Lager:    M<sup>c</sup>Ewan's, Foster's, Stella Artois, Grolsch
Cider:    Woodpecker, Strongbow
Other:    Guinness
Sandwiches only available at lunchtime
Jukebox, Darts, Cribbage

## YE OLDE WHITE HARTE — SCOTTISH AND NEWCASTLE

Undoubtedly one of Hull's most historic buildings, there can be few public houses that can boast such a history as this establishment. It is thought that the White Harte Inn was built c.1550 by Thomas Alured, a

*Ye Olde White Harte*                                                    *Adam Stewart*

former Mayor of Hull. Upon his death it passed to his grandson, John, who was one of the 59 judges who signed King Charles I's death warrant. The building was reputed to be the house of Hull's military governors, one of whom, Sir John Hotham, by virtue of his official position, was keeper of one of the largest military arsenals in the country. It was on St George's Day 1642 that King Charles arrived at Beverley Gate not far from Ye Olde White Harte, and asked admittance to the town. Sir John realised that the King would most certainly want to relieve the town of its arsenal and called a council of war in the upstairs oak room where it was resolved to refuse the King entry. Since that day this room has become known as the Plotting Parlour or Chamber. Charles, proclaiming Hotham a traitor, withdrew to Beverley. Thus the first blow of the English Civil War was struck.

The room is also thought to have been the setting for another later plot in December 1688. It was rumoured that the military governor of the day, the Catholic Lord Langdale, was planning, along with other Catholics, to seize all the town's Protestant officers. Fortunately these officers, led by Fort Major Barrat and Captain Copley, heard of the plan, and in a reversal of fortune seized the Catholics instead, including Lord Langdale, in an operation planned with such secrecy and surprise that no blood was shed. Some accounts state that Barrat's and Copley's plan was conceived in the White Harte: others claim that it was there that these events culminated.

The anniversary of the event was celebrated on 4 December for some 80 or so years afterwards by the ringing of all the town's church bells to commemorate what became known as Town Taking Day.

The building was badly damaged by fire, reputedly in 1790, and it seems likely that it was from this time that the house was first licensed. The first Hull directory (1791) shows a John Clarkson trading as a victualler at 25 Silver Street and he is recorded in 1803 at this address, trading as the White Harte Inn. John Clarkson also acted as Hull's Chief Constable, and had 15 other officers under his command. At this time the constabulary was unpaid and needed a secondary occupation to sustain a living, and this remained the case until the establishment of salaried officers in 1836. In 1881, Ye Olde White Harte Company was formed and the house was renovated. It is worth mentioning here in common with other *olde* hostelries of the town that the prefix '*ye*' actually means '*the*' and is an incorrect transcription resulting from Old English manuscripts using the letter similar to '*y*' to signify '*th*'.

Various items of antiquity have been found over the years including swords from the Civil War, and on 30 September 1937 workmen working on the roof void of the inn discovered a secret room containing the skull of a woman, several bones and the jawbone of a child. Foul play was ruled out almost immediately (the skull was on a mantle-shelf), and a pathologist concluded that these were probably specimens used by a medical student. The skull of the unfortunate woman, nicknamed Freda, is still on display in the pub.

This house was one of the last bastions of male chauvinism until, in 1969, the landlord decided that escorted ladies would be allowed to use one part of the downstairs bar-room, which would eventually become a sort of mixed bar. Today, the Plotting Parlour with its wonderful oak panelling and not-so-secret door forms part of the pub's restaurant, and the downstairs through-bar, with its flagged floors, ancient open fire place and stained glass windows, plays host to a wide cross-section of humanity with tourists much in evidence.

Silver Street takes its name from the highly regarded silversmiths who traded here in the 17th century: examples of their work are extremely rare and much sought after.

Bitter: Theakston XB<sup>cc</sup>, Old Peculier<sup>cc</sup>, N° 3 Trad<sup>cc</sup>, IPA Trad<sup>cc</sup>,
M<sup>c</sup>Ewan's Export, Exhibition
Lager: M<sup>c</sup>Ewan's, Beck's, Coors Extra Gold
Cider: Dry Blackthorn, Autumn Gold
Other: Guinness
Bar meals and sandwiches are available Monday — Sunday, 11.30am — 2.00pm. The restaurant serves meals Monday — Sunday 12.00 noon — 2.00pm and is also available for private party bookings in the evening.
Beer garden
CAMRA recommended 1993

## THE SAILMAKERS ARMS — VAUX

How aptly named! Ship's chandlers can be traced back to this site since the 1850s when it was occupied by a Thomas Canby, who plied his trade fitting out the numerous sailing ships berthed in Hull. By the 1860s, E S Humphrey and Company were the occupants, followed by Rayment and Sharp in the 1870s, and E E Sharp and Sons by 1930. It was converted by local solicitor, John Eastwood, into a public house and named The Sailmakers Arms in February 1988.

For so young a pub it has had a succession of owners, including Old English Inns, which became part of Great Northern Leisure, before passing over to Vaux Brewers in June 1991. Its function room is the old sail loft and it is reputed that a death by hanging took place here at the turn of the century. In more recent times it has won three awards from Hull Civic Society for the floral display which adorns its beer garden.

Bitter:  Wards Best, The Governor[cc](g)
Lager:   Carlsberg Export, Labatt's, Stella Artois
Cider:   Strongbow, Woodpecker
Other:   Hull Brewery Mild[cc], Guinness
Bar meals and sandwiches are available here Monday — Sunday, 12.00 noon — 2.30pm
Jukebox, Darts
CAMRA recommended, 1993

*The Sailmakers Arms*       *Adam Stewart*

## YE OLDE BLACK BOY — PUBMASTER

This famous hostelry's origins can be traced back to 1331 and over the centuries it has enjoyed many different guises: corn merchants, insurance brokers, private residence, wine and spirit merchants, fish shop and brothel! Carter's Coffee Shop opened on this site in 1730 (Coffee Shops also sold beer in those days) and it is thought that it was then that the house first became known as the Black Boy. The owner was reputed to have employed the services of a high caste Moroccan boy as a novelty to try and increase trade.

Another theory is that the pub is named after Charles II whose dark swarthy looks earned him the nickname of 'Black Boy' during the period in which Oliver Cromwell was Lord Protector of England (1653-58). Royalists would raise their glasses and drink a toast to the 'Black Boy' whilst Charles II was in exile in France and Holland (1651-1660). The

pub had three underground passages leading to the River Hull, possibly much used by smugglers in former times, although it has been suggested to me that the tunnels which this house had in common with other public houses were, in fact, sewers.

*Ye Olde Black Boy*
*Adam Stewart*

12

Landlords of inns often acted as ticket sellers for the many ships which sailed out of Hull. The 1826 Hull directory has the pub's licensee, George North, as agent for the 'York old butter sloops' which sailed to and from the town every six days: *'The Musters attend at the Black Boy, 151 High Street.'*

The Black Boy was noted for cock-fighting in former times and it is also reputed to be haunted: furniture and effects have been witnessed moving on many occasions, and a ghost of a Cavalier nicknamed Charlie is said to emerge through the cellar hatch door. The pub has two bars which display reminders of the slave trade but it must be stated here that Hull was never a slave port and this could not have been a place where slaves were sold. Indeed, further down High Street is the birthplace of William Wilberforce, born in 1759. He entered Parliament in 1780, championed the campaign for the abolition of slavery and became one of the country's leading reformers. Wilberforce House is now a museum and is well worth a visit.

At the time of writing, plans are in hand to convert part of the Black Boy's first floor into an eating area. Bar meals are envisaged to be served Monday — Saturday, 12.00 noon — 3.00pm, 5.30pm — 8.00pm.

High Street, Hull's main medieval street, was once also known as Hull Street after the river which flows nearby. It is a treasure-trove of local history. Other places to visit are Maister House with its magnificent staircase, now a National Trust property, Hull Streetlife Museum, and Hull and East Riding Museum.

Bitter:   Tetleys[cc], Blacksheep Special[cc](g), Clark's Festival[cc](g),
             Mitchell's ESB[cc](g), Hambleton Porter[cc](g), Chainmaker
             Stonehenge[cc](g) N.B.: guest beers changed regularly
Lager:   Labatt's
Cider:   Dry Blackthorn
Other:   Guinness
Darts, Dominoes, Cribbage

## YE OLDE BLUE BELL — SAMUEL SMITH'S

At least 250 years old, it began its life as a popular coaching and carriers' inn. The 1791 Hull directory shows that routes had been well established throughout Yorkshire and Lincolnshire. The Patrington Coach for example:

*'Sets off from Edward Thorp's in Patrington every Tuesday and Friday morning at Six o'clock, arrives at the Blue Bell in the Market Place, Hull,*

*at Ten; returns at Five in the evening in Summer and Four in Winter. Fare in the Summer, 2s 6d, Winter 3s.'*

The Blue Bell was a common name for coaching inns, a name probably derived from a sporting connection. In the days before the Reformation a prize of a bell was given to the winner of competitions.

On one of the worst nights of the Blitz during the Second World War fires raged all around the building. The staircase caught alight, but Martin Cross, the landlord, managed to extinguish them. He also kept a parrot called — you guessed it — Polly, which saw 25 years of service and drank gin and tonic. A relative, also called Martin, had his own brewery in Osborne Street, which was sold to Messrs Gleadow and Dibb in 1887. Now a Samuel Smith's house, Ye Olde Blue Bell is approached through a quaint white-washed alley. One of its two bars has an unusual motif of what appears to be a mythological figure. This may be associated with Classical deities such as Saturn and Ceres who were identified with agriculture, but it is more likely to be of Celtic origin.

The pub's former stables are now used as the Blue Bell's cellar.

Bitter:  Old Brewery[cc], Museum Strong[cc]
Lager:  Ayingerbräu, Ayingerbräu D Pils
Cider:  Sam Smith's Cider Reserve
Other:  Sam Smith's Dark Mild, Sam Smith's Extra Stout
Bar meals and sandwiches are available Monday — Saturday, 12.00 noon — 2.00pm
Pool, Dominoes, Darts, Jukebox
CAMRA recommended (1993)
**N.B.**  This house is closed Sunday lunchtime

## YE OLDE CORN EXCHANGE — BASS

Its history can be traced back to 1788 when it was called the Excise Coffee House, although there is evidence which suggests it may have been known as the Pig and Whistle before this date. By 1803 it was under the proprietorship of William Soulby and it is he who is credited with

*Ye Olde Corn Exchange*                                                                 *Adam Stewart*

re-naming it the Old Corn Exchange c.1820. He did this in honour of the generations of Yorkshire farmers and merchants who met to buy and sell corn. Much of this business was conducted in local hostelries over 'a jug', with a shake of a hand, a very civilised way of doing business, I think. Hull's Corn Exchange, now the Hull and East Riding Museum in the High Street, was opened in 1856 and stood on the site of the much earlier Custom House. Upon his departure in December 1827, William Soulby wrote:

*'The proprietor returns his most sincere thanks to the Farmers, Cornfactors, Millers and those frequenting this establishment for past favours. At the same time he begs to inform them that the Old Corn Exchange in the centre of the Market Place will continue open for the dispatch of business every Tuesday and Friday from eleven o'clock in the forenoon until half-past one in the afternoon . . .'*

The pub, nicknamed Percy's Palace in honour of long-standing former landlord Percy Johnson, who was vice-chairman of Hull Kingston Rovers and a veteran of seven Australian tours, had underground passages leading to the River Hull. One of these was opened up in recent times but the only object of any interest found was an old empty green beer bottle from William Wheatley's former brewery in Mytongate. The bottle is still in the possession of the pub. Along with many other public houses within Hull its two bars contain a good collection of rugby memorabilia and it was the first public house within Hull to become a member of CALM.

Bitter: Bass<sup>cc</sup>, Stones<sup>cc</sup>, Worthington Best<sup>cc</sup>
Lager: Carling Black Label, Tennent's Pilsner, Tennent's Extra
Cider: Autumn Gold, Dry Blackthorn
Other: Bass Mild<sup>cc</sup>, Guinness
Bar meals and sandwiches are available Monday — Saturday, 12.00 noon — 2.00pm

## KING WILLIAM — FREEHOUSE

John Hellier, described as the proprietor of a Coffee House and News Subscription Rooms, operated from this site in the early 1830s. He was granted a wine and spirit licence on 22 October 1834 and began trading as the Commercial Coffee House. Ownership had passed over to Henry Dean by 1840, and the name was changed to Dean's Coffee House. He was probably a relative of Francis Dean, wine and spirit merchant, who held the licence for the Kingston Hotel, also in the Market Place. Dean

*King William*
Jonathon White

operated hot and
cold vapour baths
as a sideline. It
was renamed the
King William by
1860 because of
its proximity to
William      III's
statue.

The statue of William of Orange, 'opened' on 4 December 1734, was sculpted by Peter Scheemaker. Legend has it that Scheemaker promptly committed suicide after the unveiling ceremony because he had forgotten to include the stirrups. This is, in fact, a myth as he died in 1781 at the ripe old age of 90. You will notice that William is not saddled, so therefore would have no need for stirrups; he is, of course, riding the horse bare-backed, wearing sandals in a classical pose, reminiscent of Greek and Roman styles, popular at the time. However, what is true is that King Billy, as the locals fondly call both him and the pub, dismounts from his horse every night when he *hears* the historic Trinity Church clock strike midnight, knocks on the door and asks for a pint!

The Prince of Orange was viewed as the great Protestant saviour of the people from the much disliked Catholic James II. Hull's governor, Lord

17

Langdale, of strong Catholic persuasion, prepared the town for a siege, fearing the Prince of Orange's arrival by sea from Holland with an army of some 15,000 troops of deliverance in 1688. The Prince, however, landed at a village called Broxholme in Devon.

Hull City Council placed a compulsory purchase order on this house in 1975 and, after much argument between its former owners, Mansfield Brewery, and the Council, it was closed in the summer of 1991. It reopened on 30 March 1992 as a bastion of real ale dispensed by Alex Craig, a devotee and leading light of CAMRA. Curiously the pub's sign displays the wrong William. The portrait is of William IV who reigned 1830-1837. Its present utilitarian interior displays many posters of independent brewers. We cannot, however, leave this house without paying a visit . . . another sort of visit, to the loo's beneath King Billy's statue. These fine Edwardian gentlemen's toilets by B Finch and Company of Lambeth have recently been immortalised by Lucinda Lambton's television exposé of great British sanitary arrangements. More than a penny was spent here in their construction. Marbled urinals, mosaic floor, fine brass fitments and see-through cisterns all add to their splendour.

Bitter: Old Mill[cc], King Billy Bitter[cc], Timothy Taylor's Landlord[cc], Butter Knowle Conciliation[cc](g), Blacksheep Special[cc](g), Malton Double Chance[cc](g), Rooster Yankee[cc](g), N.B.: guest beers changed regularly
Lager: Ayingerbräu
Cider: Westons Old Rosie
Other: Hull Brewery Mild[cc], Selby Old Tom[cc]
Darts, Dominoes

## EARL DE GREY

This house was probably called the Junction Dock Tavern c.1830 or stood on a spot very close to it. The Junction Dock, later re-named Princes Dock, was opened in 1829. By the mid-1860s it appears the pub had become the Earl De Grey, having been named after George Frederick Samuel Robinson, Earl De Grey and Ripon. He was born at 10 Downing Street in 1827 (his father was Viscount Goderich, Prime Minister) and he came to Hull in 1852 as the young Lord Goderich offering himself as Liberal candidate in the general election of that year. He was duly elected, only to be un-ceremoniously unseated shortly afterwards, having been found guilty of breaking the law governing the conduct of elections.

Not to be thwarted he re-entered Parliament as MP for Huddersfield and went on to become Under Secretary of War in 1859 and later

*Earl de Grey*                                                                                        *Adam Stewart*

Governor General of India and First Lord of the Admiralty. Honour upon honour was bestowed upon him and he was created the Marquis of Ripon in 1871. In 1863 he accepted the honorary office of High Steward of Hull, thus renewing his links with the town, an event which was highly popular with the townsfolk. He died in 1909.

The inn is reputed to have been frequented by the press gangs who would ply their victims with copious amounts of liquor, then smuggle them to a waiting ship via the pub's underground passage which leads to the dock. However, I consider this to be highly unlikely as the press gangs operated during the period following the outbreak of the French Revolution in 1789 and the end of the Napoleonic Wars, 1815.

This is perhaps Hull's most colourful pub, renowned throughout the world for being popular with ladies of the street and all manner of 'rough and toughs' in not so distant times. The saying goes that you needed a passport and a luger to gain entry, a reputation, I must state, that it does not deserve.

A popular attraction was a pair of macaws, called Ringo and Cha Cha, introduced by Laurence Dexter, a former landlord in the 1960s. The birds swore like troopers and saw many years of service. Sadly, following a burglary at the pub in 1977, Ringo swore once too often and was throttled, his body thrown into the gents' urinal (from the gutter to the gutter). The birds were, in fact, kept in the gents at night-time so that the landlord could get a good night's sleep. Ringo was laid to rest amongst the newly mixed concrete of the dual carriageway opposite which was under construction at the time. The miscreants who had done this dastardly deed were caught and were brought up before the 'beak'. Cha Cha died soon afterwards, reputedly of a broken heart. Ringo II was introduced 18 months after Ringo I's demise, but he too is now a deceased parrot, having fallen off a curtain and cracking a rib.

The 'Earl' has recently undergone major refurbishment by its new proprietor, Robert Mays, whose family also control Hull's Tower Night Club.

Castle Street was once called Burford Street but was renamed after the prominent early 19th-century builder, George Castle.

Bitter: Tetley$^{cc}$, Boddingtons$^{cc}$
Lager: Castlemaine XXXX, Löwenbräu
Cider: Strongbow, Woodpecker
Other: Tetley Mild, Guinness
Sandwiches freshly made, to order
Jukebox, Bed and Breakfast


## THE ROYAL WILLIAM — TOM COBLEY

This house probably owns the record for the most name-changed public house of note within Hull. A pub newly licensed as The Board, a common name for inns and taverns, occupied this site c.1800. Its origins date back to manorial times when heavy oak boards were used to bring in great joints of meat to feed the household, and the word has over the years become a term associated with accommodation and food, boarding house, board and lodgings et al. It is also a term long-used to indicate the existence of a liquor licence of an un-named licensed property, a practice still adopted.

By 1826 this house was trading as the Gilded Gallon and is listed in Hull directories as the Gilt Gallon during the 1830s. Its name was changed to the King William during the mid-1840s, its landlord, William Smith, presiding over two more name changes: the George IV, listed in the 1851 directory, becoming The Royal William c.1858. The pub was closed because of structural problems in November 1980 and was subsequently redeveloped by pub operators, Inn Leisure. During this period the pub became known locally as The Pie and Pint. This house has recently become part of the Tom Cobley empire, a pub chain which specialises in real ale. Let us hope that this intimate wood-panelled,

20

*The Royal William*
Jonathon White

beamed, one-bar pub does not have to suffer the indignity of any further name changes!

Waterhouse Lane was formerly known as Tanhouse Lane and takes its present name from Hull's waterworks which stood at its northern end in the 17th century.

Bitter:    Theakston XB[cc], Theakston Best[cc], Directors[cc], Flowers[cc], Boddingtons[cc](g), Wadworths 6X[cc](g)
Lager:    Carling Black Label, Beck's
Cider:    Woodpecker, Strongbow
Other:    Bass Mild[cc], Murphy's
Sandwiches are available every session throughout the week. Bar meals are currently on offer 12.00 noon — 2.00pm with the exceptions of Wednesday and Sunday. They are also available during the evening although service times vary.

# DID YOU KNOW?

The Four in Hand on Holderness Road was once the site of another pub called The Four Alls and had four statues set into its corners:
A King, 'I rule all'
A Priest, 'I pray for all'
A Soldier, 'I fight for all'
John Bull, 'I pay for all'.

**********

The Polar Bear, Spring Bank, stands opposite Hull's old Zoological Gardens which contained a polar bear pit. The original pub stood further down Spring Bank and once boasted a private museum which housed amongst other things an ostrich, a pair of lions, and a 15-foot elephant called Old Tom.

**********

Talking of elephants, the Elephant and Castle on Holderness Road is so called because it harks back to the days of the British Raj in India. The Castle or Howdah was a seat placed on the back of an elephant.

**********

One of the most popular drinks served to students at Hull University Students Union is called a 'Purple Nasty'. This consists of lager, cider and blackcurrant cordial, commonly called a snakebite and black, or diesel elsewhere in the town.

**********

Parkers, formerly the Newington, Walton Street, and Rayners, formerly the Star and Garter, Hessle Road, are both named after long-standing popular landlords: Ernest Parker and Henry Rayner.

**********

You could buy a dozen bottles of champagne at Ye Olde White Harte in 1883 for 44 old shillings, which is equivalent to £2.20 now. The same today would cost you £275!

**\*\*\*\*\*\*\*\*\***

Amongst Hull's most unusually named former licensed premises were:
Jack on a Cruise, North Street
Tally Ho, Bond Street
Tom Coffin, Humber Street
Indian Chief, Blackfriargate
Labour in Vain, Humber Street
March of Intellect, Waterworks Street
B Sharp, Osborne Street
Jack's Return, Grimsby Lane.

**\*\*\*\*\*\*\*\*\***

The Pelican, James Reckitt Avenue, received its name because it was built adjacent to Earle's Cement Recreation Ground, and the company's emblem was a pelican.

**\*\*\*\*\*\*\*\*\***

The most popular name for a pub recorded in the district of Hull is The Ship, excluding 'Ships' which carried additional names, *e.g.* Ship Molly, It is believed there were 16 Ship Inns during the 1800s. We are now left with only three, excluding those that have been renamed. These are:
The Ship Inn, Ann Watson Street
The Ship Inn, Hodgson Street
The Ship, Church Street, Sutton.

**\*\*\*\*\*\*\*\*\***

The Good Old Days...
Dr Jackson, objecting to a renewal of a licence in 1897 and speaking on behalf of the Chief Constable, submitted this to Hull Magistrates:

*'Bean Street in itself was 860 yards long, and contains at present 17 licensed houses — 15 beer-off licences, one fully licensed house and one beer-on licence. If they took a radius of 20, 40 and 200 yards, they found one beer-off in every 20 yards, four in 40 yards and eight in 200 yards.'*

# Around The Bridges

(Map not to scale)

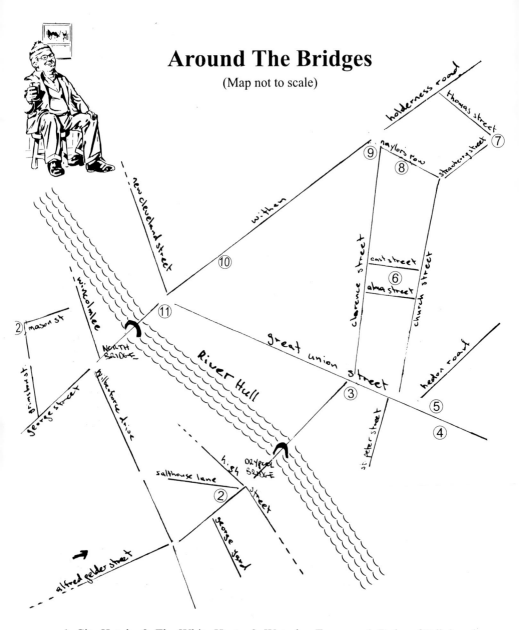

1. City Hotel   2. The White Hart   3. Waterloo Tavern   4. Duke of Edinburgh
5. Victoria Dock Tavern   6. Red Lion   7. The Kingston Arms
8. The Blacksmiths Arms   9. Windmill Hotel   10. Plimsoll Ship Hotel
11. Kings Arms   12. Old English Gentleman

# HOWARD'S WAY (Part Two) — AROUND THE BRIDGES

| | | |
|---|---|---|
| City Hotel | Lowgate | Tel: 223402 |
| The White Hart | Alfred Gelder Street | Tel: 228136 |
| Waterloo Tavern | Great Union Street | Tel: 228306 |
| Duke of Edinburgh | De la Pole Street | Tel: 225382 |
| Victoria Dock Tavern | Great Union Street | Tel: 26094 |
| Red Lion | Clarence Street | Tel: 24773 |
| The Kingston Arms | Thomas Street | Tel: 26376 |
| The Blacksmiths Arms | Naylors Row | Tel: 223475 |
| Windmill Hotel | Witham | Tel: 24623 |
| Plimsoll Ship Hotel | Witham | Tel: 25995 |
| Kings Arms | Witham | Tel: 28096 |
| Old English Gentleman | Mason Street | Tel: 24659 |

## CITY HOTEL — BASS

Licensed premises have stood on this site since the 1840s. During the course of its chequered history it started life as the City of London Arms, shortened to the City Arms, and became known as the Town Hall Vaults (1860s) and the Tiger No. 2 (1870s) . . . there were six Tigers in the town owned by George Stevenson, each one numbered:

| | |
|---|---|
| The Tiger, Waterworks Street (original) | No. 1 |
| The Town Hall Vaults, Lowgate, became | No. 2 |
| 27 Church Street, Sculcoates, became | No. 3 |
| The Golden Cup, Mytongate, became | No. 4 |
| The Ferry Boat, Wincolmlee, became | No. 5 |
| The Labour in Vain, Humber Street, became | No. 6 |

25

*City Hotel* *Adam Stewart*

A most enterprising fellow, I think. It reverted to the City Arms at the turn of the century before being demolished during the development of Alfred Gelder Street. The present building was built for Hewitt Brothers, brewers of Grimsby, in 1905 and opened as a first-class hotel, although this venture proved to be short-lived.

Its name reflects Hull's status as a city bestowed upon the town by Queen Victoria in 1897. This honour was a cause of great pride to the townsfolk at the time and remains so today. The pub is one of the few houses which displays the insignia of three crowns, symbol of the City. The origin of the coat of arms (its heraldic description is: Azure, three ducal coronets in gold) is uncertain. It is thought it probably dates from Edward III's visit in 1331, when he was entertained by his good friend, William de la Pole. Before leaving he granted Hull, by charter, the right to elect a mayor and four bailiffs to govern the town's affairs, William de la Pole, being the first mayor.

Today the pub retains all its Edwardian splendour but its former bedrooms and function suites are now occupied by Hull City Council Town Clerk's Department Computer Services.

Lowgate was the back street to the more important High Street and therefore known as low. It was also called Market Gate because Hull's market was originally held in this area.

Bitter: Bass[cc], Stones[cc]
Lager: Carling Black Label, Tennent's Pilsner
Cider: Dry Blackthorn
Other: Bass Mild[cc], Guinness
Sandwiches only, available at lunch time
Darts, Dominoes, Cribbage, Jukebox


## THE WHITE HART — MANSFIELD

The first reference I have been able to find to this house dates back to 1826 when a J Sawden held the licence, although it is probably much older. At that time The White Hart was listed as occupying No. 11 Salthouse Lane. As the name *salt* indicates, a salt house was a place where salt was stored, then a highly prized commodity. The area was once surrounded by fields and common land stretching as far as the approach to North Bridge, which had become a popular haunt of hunters.

The pub's name is derived from a portion of the arms of Richard II (1367-1400). The citizens of Hull had great cause to be grateful to Richard II for he bestowed many favours upon the town through his association with Michael de la Pole whose home was not far from the inn.

Inns were often used as a venue for political meetings particularly at

*The White Hart*                                                        *Adam Stewart*

election time and the White Hart was no exception. Voters were enticed to vote for candidates in exchange for a liberal supply of free ale. A crowded meeting was held here in 1839, in which many speeches were made, *'all eulogistic of the principles of Chartism and condemnatory of the conduct of the middle and higher classes'*.

The original building was demolished in 1902 and rebuilt. It would be nice to say that this reconstruction is now a monument to one of the finest Victorian bars in the county but, as Victoria died in 1901, we must settle for Victorian style. Part of this pub's bar is semi-circular, topped with mahogany, and is surrounded by fine green and gold glazed tile work. The whole effect is complete with magnificent craftsman-made mahogany showcases back of bar. This former gin palace displays a variety of unusual objects including what appears to be a very early form of carpet cleaner, and plenty of stuffed stag heads and stag horns adorn its walls.

Bitter:   Riding[cc], Old Baily[cc], Mansfield
Lager:   Marksman, Foster's
Cider:   Strongbow, Woodpecker
Other:   Riding Mild[cc], Guinness, Murphy's
Bar meals and sandwiches are available Monday — Friday, 12.00 noon — 2.00pm
Pool, Darts, Dominoes, Jukebox, Sky TV

## WATERLOO TAVERN — AYLWARD LEISURE

Standing at the beginning of the old Hedon Turnpike, the Waterloo takes its name from the great battle in which Napoleon met his match in 1815. It also appears to have been first licensed from this time, the pub's first landlord, Matthew Smith, describing it as a naval rendezvous. The Waterloo Tavern enjoys the nicknames of the 'Old Bull and Bush' or 'Bush', for which there is no apparent reason, although, I am told, the pub was once surrounded by scrubland. The Romans were known to have planted grape vines outside their wine taverns to indicate a place which sold liquid refreshment. The vine I suppose could be construed as being a bush, but somehow I do not think this was the case here! It was closed by its former owners, Courage Limited, at the beginning of 1992 and re-opened on 15 October 1992 under new ownership, having been totally refurbished. A ghostly presence is reported to have annoyed artistes appearing on stage here over many years.

The Battle of Waterloo was to be Napoleon Bonaparte's last. Bonaparte, hero of the French, had wreaked havoc throughout the whole of Europe and had won many famous tactical military victories in his

*Waterloo Tavern*                                                    *Jonathon White*

attempt to create a greater France. Ranged against Napoleon's 128,000 men and 344 cannon stood the Allied total of 200,000 men, with nearly 500 cannon, under the command of Arthur Wellesley, 1st Duke of Wellington, and the Prussian Commander, Gerhard Blücher. Initial skirmishes took place mid-June 1815 with both sides dispatching troops to cover each other's flanks and rear. The final battle took place on 18 June 1815, at Waterloo in Belgium, Napoleon's 72,000 available men outnumbering Wellington's 68,000 men-at-arms. Midway through the battle, Blücher appeared with 100,000 men on Napoleon's right flank and it was all over. Bonaparte's troops were routed and he himself exiled to St Helena.

The phrase *to meet one's Waterloo* relates directly to this battle and means a disastrous or crushing defeat.

Bitter:  Bass[cc], Stones[cc], Theakston Old Peculier[cc]
Lager:  Tennent's Extra, Tennent's Pilsner, Carling Black Label, Tennent's LA
Cider:  Strongbow, Woodpecker
Other:  Bass Mild, Guinness
Bar meals and sandwiches are available 12.00 noon — 2.00pm, 6.00pm — 8.00pm
Jukebox, Pool, Dominoes, Darts, Cribbage, Sky TV
**N.B.**This house is closed Monday and Tuesday lunch. No food available Sundays.

## DUKE OF EDINBURGH — PUBMASTER

Standing opposite the former Victoria Dock Church Basin (the dock was opened in 1850), this house was originally known as the Gate Beer House, c.1820. Its name was changed in the mid-1880s to the Dock Coffee House. Queen Victoria's second eldest son, Alfred Ernest Albert, Duke of Edinburgh, came to Hull in 1884 to lay the foundation stone of the new wing of Hull's Royal Infirmary in Prospect Street (now demolished). The pub was purchased by the Hull Brewery Company on 3 February 1892 and the new owners promptly renamed it in honour of this royal event. One of Hull's most famous sons, David Whitfield, an international singer, was brought up just around the corner from the pub. At the time of writing it is reported that this hostelry is due to be demolished in two years time to facilitate a new road . . . sacrilege!

De la Pole Street is named after Hull's most famous and influential medieval merchant family who used their vast wealth and

*Duke of Edinburgh*
*Jonathon White*

30

power to ingratiate themselves with all the kings of England between the reigns of Edward III and Henry VIII. Particularly powerful were William de la Pole, first Mayor of Hull and Baron of the Exchequer, his son Michael, who was Admiral of the Fleet in the North and Lord Chancellor of England and who was raised to the peerage as Earl of Suffolk. Suffolk Palace, the family home, was situated on the present site of Hull's main Post Office in Lowgate. The last Earl of Suffolk, Edmund, was beheaded by order of Henry VIII in 1513.

Bitter:   Tetley[cc]
Lager:   Castlemaine XXXX, Labatt's
Cider:   Dry Blackthorn
Other:   Tetley Mild[cc], Guinness, Murphy's
Jukebox, Pool, Darts, Dominoes
**N.B.**   Closed lunchtimes

*Victoria Dock Tavern*
*Jonathon White*

## VICTORIA DOCK TAVERN — CENTURY INNS

Formerly the Albion, it was built by local brewer Simon Cook in the late 1820s. The Albion took its name from a famous sailing ship of its day, though Albion is also the Latin name for England. Its name was changed to the Victoria Dock Tavern in the 1840s, reflecting the construction of Victoria Dock which was then being built. The house commanded a fine view of Hull's Citadel.

The Citadel was constructed in 1540 during the reign of Henry VIII and began at the mouth of the harbour where one of its heaviest fortifications, the South Blockhouse, was situated. Its walls extended to the North Blockhouse at Witham and there was a castle in the middle. The North Blockhouse was demolished in 1801, the Castle in 1863 and the South Blockhouse in 1864.

A small secret room was once discovered at this pub whilst alterations were being made to the landlord's accommodation. When opened it was found to contain only a table. The room was rumoured to be the setting of much skull-duggery and it was suggested that grave robbers had once brought their victims here from the former St Peter's graveyard opposite the pub. Public houses were formerly a popular venue for inquests. It is said that this house is haunted by the ghost of an old donkey greaser who is perhaps spending more time here in death than he had bargained for!

Great Union Street is so called because it provides a link (union) between Witham and Clarence Street, and the 'Great' distinguishes it from another, less important, Union Street.

Bitter:   Stones[cc], Bass[cc], Tetley[cc]
Lager:   Carling Black Label, Tennent's Pilsner, Tennent's LA
Cider:   Strongbow, Woodpecker
Other:   Bass Mild[cc], Guinness
Sandwiches are available to order
Pool, Darts, Dominoes, Cribbage

## RED LION — BASS

This house was built for Moor and Robson, brewers, in 1939 as a replacement for the old Red Lion which dated from the mid-1800s, stood 50 yards away on Church Street, and was destroyed in a bombing raid during the Second World War. The present Red Lion holds the unique distinction of being an island unto itself, bordered by four streets: East Street, Clarence Street, Alma Street and Church Street. I am told that

*Red Lion*                                              *Jonathon White*

hidden behind the false ceiling of this pub lies the remnants of an old wrought-iron bar facade which contains motifs of all the signs of the Zodiac.

Moor and Robson were one of Hull's great brewing concerns and operated out of magnificent premises in Raywell Street known as the Crown Brewery. In 1888 Hull United Breweries, principally an amalgamation of both the Moor and the Robson breweries, came into existence. Peter Robson had his brewery in Waterworks Street and Henry Moor traded out of Raywell Street, although an earlier brewery was founded in Mytongate by Sarah Moor. Almost immediately Hull United Breweries became known as Moor and Robson. The new company prospered and several acquisitions were made, so increasing their large enterprise. By 1960 they had 138 houses but were taken over in 1962 by Hewitt Brothers, brewers, of Grimsby.

Bitter:   Tetley[cc], Stones[cc]
Lager:   Carling Black Label, Tennent's Pilsner
Cider:   Woodpecker
Other:   Guinness
Sandwiches available by request
Jukebox, Darts, Dominoes, Cribbage

## THE KINGSTON ARMS — FREE HOUSE

Standing in the heart of the former Strawberry Garden district, this house was built as a replacement for an older public house originally known as the Gardeners Arms, c.1800. By the mid-1820s it was trading as the Crooked Billet, its sign consisting of two pieces of wood, crossed in the shape of a St Andrew's Cross, the symbol of Saint Julien, patron saint of travellers, who was supposed to have attended the needs of the weary. During the 1830s the inn was variously known as the Sportsman and the Red House.

The present public house was erected in 1850 during the layout of Thomas Street. Its sign displays the three crowns, emblem of the City. This was Percy Johnson's (of Hull Kingston Rovers fame) first public house and regulars will remember his mascot, Pud Saddington, named in honour of his good friend, William Saddington, another former Rovers star. Percy tells me that William would often entertain his customers with his fine singing voice and good humour. The pub stands alone now, with most of Thomas Street demolished, although this is one place where you will never feel alone. Its friendly atmosphere is legendary.

Strawberry Gardens appear to have been established c.1800 and could accommodate upwards of 200 persons. They reputedly contained a small

*The Kingston Arms*                                                              *Jonathon White*

vinery, 91 apple trees, 44 cherry trees, 29 pear trees, 12 plum trees, 500 gooseberry and currant bushes, 7 strawberry beds, arbours, skittle and quoit pitches. A sort of early 'pick your own', I suppose, and proved at their conception to be very popular. By 1820 the area had degenerated and become the resort of the lowest and vilest blackguards in the district, drunken quarrels were often reported and the landlords of local hostelries were frequently paraded before local magistrates for providing the cause. By 1850 these picturesque gardens had all but disappeared.

Bitter:    Bass[cc], Worthington Best[cc], Stones[cc]
Lager:    Carling Black Label, Tennent's
Cider:    Woodpecker, Strongbow
Other:    Bass Mild[cc], Guinness
Sandwiches are available Monday — Thursday, bar meals and sandwiches served Friday lunch
Jukebox, Darts, Dominoes, Pool


## THE BLACKSMITHS ARMS — VAUX

Established c. 1840 and originally known as the Iron Moulders Arms, this pub is much changed from the days when iron and brass founder Thomas

*The Blacksmiths Arms*                                                    *Jonathon White*

35

Price seems to have held its first licence. It is known that it once stood next to a blacksmith's shop and was in all probability run by the smith as a secondary occupation. It was quite usual for enterprising tradesmen to supplement their livings by retailing beer, a side-line which proved, as often as not, so lucrative that it quickly became their main source of income. These houses were named after the occupations of their early owners: hence we get Carpenters Arms, Brickmakers Arms, Marrow Bone and Cleaver (Butchers), *et al.* It appears to have been renamed The Blacksmiths Arms c.1860. The new name continues the light engineering theme for which the area became popular and which remains so today.

It was one of the few public houses owned by Messrs Darley, brewers, who acquired it at the turn of the century. Darley's have now been bought by Vaux and their long established brewery has been demolished. Extensive alterations and rebuilding took place within this house in 1929. A poltergeist is said to reside here, with many articles being mysteriously moved over the years.

Naylors Row is thought to have been named after a partner of a firm of millers who traded nearby.

Bitter:   Vaux[cc], Samson[cc], Thorne Best, Vaux Pale Ale
Lager:   Labatt's, Tuborg Pilsner
Cider:   Strongbow, Woodpecker
Other:   Thorne Dark Mild[cc], Guinness
Bar meals and sandwiches are available Monday — Friday, 12.00 noon — 2.00pm. Saturday — sandwiches only.
Pool, Jukebox, Darts, Dominoes, Cribbage
The Royal Antediluvian Order of Buffaloes Lodge of King George V meet here.

## WINDMILL HOTEL — BASS

A cottage occupied this site for many years until a William Stephenson obtained a licence in 1816, trading as the North Blockhouse Mill Inn. The Blockhouse which stood nearby was part of Hull's heavily fortified Citadel and stood adjacent to Tinegate's Mill.

The area marked the beginning of the old Holderness Turnpike. It must have been a sight to behold, gazing eastward along the turnpike across what was then open farmland, the vista broken only by the occasional farmhouse and the many windmills. Sadly, we are left with only the remains of one of these mills, Rank's (later known as Eyre's Mill), itself recently incorporated to form part of a public house. It was here in 1854 that Joseph Rank of Rank Hovis McDougall fame was born. Mr Stephenson, referred to previously, later traded as The Mill, but by the mid-1820s as The Windmill.

*Windmill Hotel*
*Jonathon White*

At the turn of the 19th century the pub was owned by local pub operator and brewer, William Wheatley, who had the old cottage demolished and rebuilt in 1902 during the period in which Clarence Street was laid out. Rebuild he did! With its glazed brown tile work and motifs of windmills set over its doors it was a sight to behold. Even today, after the passage of time, it still displays the remains of its former glory. As magnificent as this house was, it became known locally as Wheatley's Folly because he had embarked on a similar project in the rebuilding of the Crown public house in nearby St Quentin's Place some years earlier and this again had to be demolished during the development of Clarence Street. Shortly after rebuilding The Windmill Hotel, Wheatley sold his brewery and public houses to Bass, Ratcliffe and Gretton, although he retained a management interest in the operation of the pub.

Bitter:   Bass$^{cc}$, Bass Light, Stones
Lager:   Carling Black Label, Tennent's Pilsner
Other:   Bass Mild, Guinness
Jukebox, Pool, Darts, Dominoes, Cribbage, Bed and Breakfast
The Royal Antediluvian Order of Buffaloes Lodges of Humber, Brunswick-Taylor and Haven meet here
**N.B.**This house is closed Tuesday lunchtime

## PLIMSOLL SHIP HOTEL
## — THE HULL BREWERY COMPANY

Built during the boom years of the Napoleonic Wars, this hostelry started life as The Ship in about 1803. Originally it had stables for 20 horses, being on a popular coaching route. It was purchased by Messrs Gleadow, Dibb and Company in 1876 and was renamed the Plimsoll Ship Hotel in honour of Samuel Plimsoll, originator of the Plimsoll Line: this is a line on the hull of a merchant ship which indicates the depth to which it may be legally loaded under specific conditions. Samuel Plimsoll (1824-1898), a prominent MP for Derby, married on the 8 October 1885 Harriet Frankish Wade, daughter of Hull timber merchant, Joseph Wade JP.

An ex-landlord was Sam Morfitt, who was a former player for Hull Kingston Rovers and one of its first stars. In 1896 he was the first Rovers player to

*Plimsoll Ship Hotel*
Jonathon White

38

represent his county and was part of the winning team which took the Yorkshire County Cup and Rugby League Championship in 1896/7.

After falling into bad repair the pub was closed in 1985 but was subsequently re-designed and re-opened by local builder, Joe Parkinson, in the spring of 1987. With its honey-coloured fine woodwork and dome set into its ceiling, the pub earned Mr Parkinson a Civic Trust Award for its skilful conversion. The Plimsoll Ship Hotel has, at the time of writing, become the first public house of the new Hull Brewery Company, being purchased in June 1992.

Witham was previously known as Blockhouse Lane, because of its proximity to the former defences on the east bank of the River Hull. It later became known as Witham after Henry Witham, a property owner of the district.

Bitter:   Hull Brewery[cc], The Governor[cc], Tetley[cc]
Lager:   Castlemaine XXXX, Skol, Löwenbräu
Cider:   Copperhead, Olde English
Other:   Hull Brewery Mild[cc], Guinness
Bar meals and sandwiches are available Monday — Friday, 12.00 noon — 2.00pm
Jukebox, Darts, Dominoes, Cribbage
CAMRA recommended 1993


## KINGS ARMS — CENTURY INNS

The original Kings Arms stood nearby and was formerly called the Wellington c.1800, being renamed the Kings Arms in the 1850s. It was purchased by Messrs Moor and Robson in the 1890s and bought from them by Hull Corporation in 1930 to facilitate a new approach road to the new North Bridge. On completion of these works, Moor and Robson commissioned the building of the present Kings Arms next to the powerhouse of the bridge.

The Arms displayed over the pub's entrance are those of Edward III and quarter three lions, first introduced by Richard I (Coeur de Lion), and three fleur-de-lis, a form of stylized lily included by Edward III in his Arms as part of his claim to the French throne. The inscription *Dieu et mon Droit* (God and my right) was first used at this time and is included in the present Arms used by the Royal family which these days quarter the three kingdoms of England, Scotland and Ireland.

Crossing the river has always been an impediment to the people of Hull and probably remains just as frustrating today as it was in medieval times when it was crossed by ferry. A six-arched bridge was first built at the time of construction of Hull's eastern wall c.1540, was replaced in 1785 by one with four arches and a central drawbridge, and again in 1870 with

*Kings Arms*

*Jonathon White*

a horizontal drawbridge designed by Martin Samuelson. He was a 19th-century shipbuilder and Sammy's Point is named after his shipyard which existed on the site. The present bridge was opened on 10 August 1931.

Bitter: Stones[cc], Tetley[cc](g)
Lager: Carling Black Label
Cider: Strongbow, Woodpecker
Other: Bass Mild[cc], Guinness
Sandwiches are available lunchtime only
Jukebox, Dartboard, Pool, Dominoes

## OLD ENGLISH GENTLEMAN — MANSFIELD

The Old English Gentleman stands on the corner of Mason Street on the periphery of Kingston Square, opposite the New Theatre. The theatre was once Hull's Assembly Rooms: the smell of greasepaint wafting across its audience for the first time in 1939 during a performance of *Me and My Girl*. The pub was originally listed as No. 22 Worship Street and was occupied by former chair-maker and hackney-gig owner, Edmund Halley, c.1831, who traded as a shopkeeper and flour dealer from these

40

*Old English Gentleman*                                    Adam Stewart

premises. He was later granted a beer-only licence. The house became the property of Martin Cross, brewers, who sold the pub to Messrs Gleadow and Dibb in 1887 at a cost of £1,500, upon their amalgamation. Nicknamed the 'O.E.G.', this house with its intimate wood-panelled through-bar displays a collection of over 130 signed photographs of artistes past and present who have appeared at the theatre. The collection was started by Ron Fewliss, licensee in the 1960s, who instigated a tradition which has been maintained ever since.

Its original pub sign depicted a man dressed in Stuart style with a spaniel on his knee, mounted . . . upon a plinth. Today the sign bears a likeness of Alfred Gelder, Hull's famous late 19th- and early 20th-century architect, an honour this true gentleman richly deserves.

Mason Street was so named after a prominent property-owning family.

Bitter:   Riding[cc], Mansfield
Lager:   M[c]Ewan's, Foster's, Stella Artois, Tennent's LA
Cider:   Strongbow
Other:   Riding Mild[cc], Guinness
Bar meals and sandwiches are available Monday — Friday, 12.00 noon — 2.30pm, 5.00pm — 7.00pm
Jukebox, Darts, Dominoes, Cribbage
CAMRA recommended 1993.

41

# THE HULL BREWERY COMPANY

The company name of Hull Brewery is synonymous with this city and all who drink in it. Its origins can be traced back to 1782 when Thomas Ward, an inn-holder, established a brewery on the corner of Posterngate and Dagger Lane in the Old Town. Following his death in 1796 the brewery passed to his son John, and, when *he* died in 1814, his sisters, Ann and Mary, inherited the business. Mary married Robert Gleadow, a shipbuilder, and after his death ownership passed over to their son, Robert Ward Gleadow, who in 1846 took William Thomas Dibb, a brewer in Mill Street, into partnership. They traded prosperously as Gleadow, Dibb and Company and in 1868 moved into new premises in Sylvester Street which they had commissioned to be built two years earlier. A period of rapid growth followed and further acquisitions were made.

Following a share issue in 1888 the board of directors decided to change the company name and the Hull Brewery Company was born. The company traded successfully through both world wars and it was eventually sold to Northern Dairies in 1972. Northern Dairies became Northern Foods and they in turn operated the business under the new company name of North Country Breweries. Mixed fortunes befell the brewery at this time and, despite huge cash injections to improve their now considerable estate, they sold the entire business to Mansfield Breweries plc in 1985. Mansfield, having their own brewery, saw no need for the brewery in Sylvester Street to be retained and so ended over 200 years of brewing in Hull. The brewery, known as The Maltings, is now a business park.

The new Hull Brewery Company was established in the winter of 1989 by Denis Armstrong in partnership with others. Denis spotted a niche in the market provided by the sad loss of the much loved Hull Brewery Mild and enlisted the help of the former Hull Brewery's last and much respected head brewer, Peter Austin, who acts as a consultant to the new firm. Together they set about re-creating the brew in premises converted from an old fish-smoking house situated in English Street. The modern plant, much of it designed by Peter himself, now also produces Hull Brewery Bitter and the stronger Governor. These beers are now marketed the length and breadth of the country. The first batch of Hull Brewery Mild was delivered from these premises to the West Hull Liberal Club on 11 December 1989.

# The Milk Run

(Map not to scale)

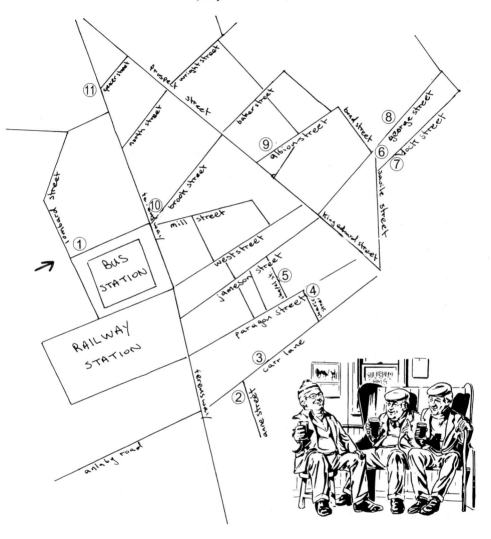

1. The Green Ginger Man   2. The King Edward VII   3. White Horse Hotel
4. The Hull Cheese   5. The Bass House   6. Dram Shop   7. Rugby Tavern
8. Manchester Hotel   9. The Institute   10. The Shire Horse   11. Monroe's

# HOWARD'S WAY (Part Three) — THE MILK RUN

| | | |
|---|---|---|
| The Green Ginger Man | Lombard Street | Tel: 224782 |
| The King Edward VII | Anne Street | Tel: 25811 |
| White Horse Hotel | Carr Lane | Tel: 24837 |
| The Hull Cheese | Paragon Street | Tel: 225314 |
| The Bass House | Chapel Street | Tel: 24407 |
| Dram Shop | George Street | Tel: 27688 |
| Rugby Tavern | Dock Street | Tel: 24759 |
| Manchester Hotel | George Street | Tel: 20261 |
| The Institute | Albion Street | Tel: 587387 |
| The Shire Horse | Ferensway | Tel: 25778 |
| Monroe's | Ferensway | Tel: 24536 |

## THE GREEN GINGER MAN — MANSFIELD

Situated near the exit of Hull's bus station, it is perhaps, by virtue of its position, the Town's most 'seen' public house.

Originally given an address in Collier Street, variously listed as No. 32 and No. 52, before the building of the coach station, it began life as the Brickmakers Arms c.1838 before being re-named the White Lion in 1867, and became a popular haunt of 'cabbies'. It was without doubt also frequented by Charles Peace, the infamous Victorian expert cat-burglar who became known as the 'Murderous Musician'. This former violin player, billed as 'The Modern Paganini', used his violin case to carry the tools of his more lucrative secondary occupation, whilst committing burglaries. After a warrant was issued for his arrest for threatening Arthur Dyson, his former lover's husband, with a gun in Sheffield, he fled to Hull with his family (where his mother lived) and established a café in Collier Street. Unbeknown to the police at this time, he had also shot and killed a policeman during a burglary in Manchester. Charles Peace returned to

Sheffield and shot dead Arthur Dyson on the evening of 29 November 1876. Now one of Britain's most wanted men, he was eventually arrested in London and kept his appointment with the hangman's noose at Armley Jail, Leeds, on 25 February 1879, having bitterly complained about the 'bloody rotten bacon' he had eaten for his last breakfast.

The entire pub was dismantled in the winter of 1933/4 and was transported to Wilberforce House by Tom Sheppard, Hull's former and well-respected Museum Curator, where it became part of a street scene. This exhibit was unfortunately lost during the Blitz.

The present building was opened on 27 August 1934 and its name changed in 1979 by its owners, North Country Breweries, to The Green Ginger Man, paying homage to Hull's most famous street. It was again extensively refurbished in 1986 and at that time boasted Hull's first satellite television which picked up music channels from around the world.

The provision of public transport forms one of the keystones of any community and Hull is blessed with having one of the finest in the country. Control of these facilities was first made in 1783 when all wheeled carriages and sedan chairs had to be licensed. Horse tramways began to appear in 1872, steam trams towards 1890, and by the end of 1900 these routes had begun to be electrified. Motor buses were

*The Green Ginger Man*    *Adam Stewart*

introduced in 1909, although this service was withdrawn between 1913-1921. Many people will remember with affection trolley buses which put in their first appearance in 1936 and their last in 1964: the last tram ran in 1945.

The town's coach station and central garage was opened in 1935 and plays host to 109 buses and 12 mini-buses operated by Kingston upon Hull City Transport, East Yorkshire Motor Transport who have staging rights at the station, and have in service 131 buses based at their Anlaby Road depot, 47 based at Hedon Road and 14 at Beverley. There are also 16 bus and coaches servicing local routes in private ownership.

Bitter:   Riding<sup>cc</sup>, Mansfield
Lager:   Foster's, Red Stripe
Cider:   Woodpecker, Strongbow
Other:   Riding Mild<sup>cc</sup>, Guinness
Bar meals and sandwiches are available Monday — Saturday, 12.00 noon — 2.00pm
Jukebox, Pool, Darts
**N.B.**   Closed Sunday lunch

## KING EDWARD VII — VAUX

Named after Queen Victoria's eldest son who became King in 1901 and died in 1910. As the Prince of Wales he features heavily in the annals of Hull's history following the Tranby Croft baccarat scandal which took place on 9 September 1890. Tranby Croft (now Hull High School for Girls) was the home of millionaire shipping owner Arthur Wilson and it was whilst the Prince was staying here that Sir William Gordon-Cumming, a wealthy aristocrat with a glittering military record, was accused of cheating over a game of cards. Gordon-Cumming, in an interview with the Prince, protested his innocence and said that he hoped that he would not believe the *'foul and abominable charges against him'*. The Prince replied, *'What can you do? There are five witnesses against you!'* To admit to the charge would have meant social ruin, and a compromise was reached in which his five accusers would remain silent about the affair in return for Gordon-Cumming's pledge never to play cards again. It was to prove a great tactical blunder on his part.

The story quickly became the gossip of staid Victorian England and, in order to save face, Gordon-Cumming brought against his protagonists an action alleging slander. The ensuing court case in June 1891, with the Prince of Wales giving evidence against this unfortunate fellow, was to prove a sensation. The jury gave their verdict for the defendants and Sir William was socially ostracised for the rest of his life. *The Times* said that he *'must leave the army, must leave his clubs and must no longer consider*

*The King Edward VII*

*himself a member of that society in which he has moved so long'.*
The King Edward VII was erected in 1957 for Messrs Darley
(brewers) and was part of Hull's Licence Planning Agreement in which
those brewers who had lost pubs during the Blitz were given the first
opportunity to build new ones. The pub is fondly known as 'Teddy's'
amongst the locals of the town.

Bitter:  Wards Sheffield Best, Samson
Lager:  Labatt's, Stella Artois
Cider:  Woodpecker, Strongbow
Other:  Darley's Mild, Guinness
Bar meals and sandwiches available Monday — Friday, 11.30am — 2.00pm
**N.B.**    Closed Sunday Lunch

## WHITE HORSE HOTEL — BASS

In common with other houses such as Red Lion, White Lion, Green
Dragon *et al*, its name has its origins in heraldry and has been depicted
on and off over the years in many royal coats of arms, being shown as a

unicorn. The introduction of the white horse to these shores dates back to the Celtic invasions of the 2nd century BC by people who left their mark on coins and hillside, such as the magnificent carved representation at Uffington.

This pub stands on the site of an older White Horse Inn. The earliest reference I have been able to find to this house is contained within the 1803 Hull directory and lists John Nunnington as the owner, a former victualler trading in Beverley Gates. The present pub was completed in spring 1957 for Messrs Worthington and Company and stands, in part, on the site of the former Imperial Hotel which was totally demolished in 1967 to make way for the Centre Hotel (now called The Portland), officially opened on 30 October 1968.

Bitter:  Stones
Lager:  Tennent's Pilsner, Carling Black Label
Cider:  Autumn Gold, Dry Blackthorn
Other:  Bass Mild, Guinness
Jukebox, Darts

*White Horse Hotel*                                    *Adam Stewart*

*The Hull Cheese*                                   Adam Stewart

## THE HULL CHEESE — MANSFIELD

This house was formerly called the Paragon Commercial Hotel, later shortened to the Paragon, and was established c.1800. Originally it had stabling and lock-up coach houses at the rear. The intimate Red Room on the first floor with its obvious connotations became infamous throughout Hull in the 1950/60's. It received its present appellation from Hull's traditional brew:

> *'Thanks to my loving host and hostess*
> *Pease,*
> *There at mine inn each night I took my ease,*
> *And there I got a cantle of Hull Cheese.'*

So wrote the former bargee and famous water poet, John Taylor, in the early 17th century whilst residing at Hull's renowned hostelry, the Kings Head, which was situated in High Street but no longer survives.

Hull Cheese was a strong local brew: *'It is much like a loaf out of a brewer's basket, it is composed of two simples, malt and water in one compound, and is cousin germane to the mightiest ale in England.'* *'He hath eaten some Hull Cheese,'* was the expression used at the time, indicating that someone was truly drunk.

John Taylor went on to become an innkeeper in London, no doubt much influenced by the 'cantle' he enjoyed during his time in Hull. What an opportunity now for some enterprising brewer to try and re-create the brew. The pub was renamed The Hull Cheese in 1975 by its then owners, the former Gilpin Group, and, having been 're-themed', became an immediate success amongst the younger drinkers of the town, at one time boasting of its position as the biggest seller of Stella Artois lager in Europe. Rock murals abound in this house. The 'Stella' may have gone, having given way to more modern drinking trends, but the 'Cheese' as it is more locally known, remains just as popular.

Paragon Street takes its name from the former Paragon Hotel.

Bitter:   Riding<sup>cc</sup>, Mansfield
Lager:    M<sup>c</sup>Ewan's, Foster's
Cider:    Woodpecker, Strongbow
Other:    Guinness
Piped CD, MTV
**N.B.**    Closed Sunday lunch.


## THE BASS HOUSE — BASS

A pub close to this site was known as the Railway Tavern (also called the Railway Tap c.1850) and its official address was 63 Paragon Street. The pub's name celebrated the recent arrival of the railway to Hull in 1840; Paragon Station was opened in 1848.

Its name was changed to the Brunswick in 1895. Great Britain's link with Brunswick, a former duchy of northern Germany, had been firmly established since the marriage of George III's eldest sister, Augusta, to the Duke of Brunswick: their daughter Caroline, was to marry George III's eldest son, George, Prince of Wales in 1795. This sad alliance was in fact bigamous as 'Prinny' had secretly married Maria Fitzherbert in 1785. Caroline was ostracised almost immediately, an act which aroused a great deal of sympathy from the British people. This strength of feeling grew the more stronger following the Prince of Wales' attempt in 1806 and again as King George IV in 1820 to prove her an adulteress. Hull's own William Wilberforce led a deputation from the House of Commons urging Caroline to relinquish all rights of being Queen: the charges were not proved.

The *Brunswick* was also a name of a famous whaling ship, a model of which is on show in Hull's Town Docks Museum. She was a full-rigged, three-master weighing 357 tons and built at Paull in 1814. Under Captain William Blyth she was the leading Hull whaler of the 1820s but lost on

*The Bass House*                                   Adam Stewart

a non-whaling voyage in 1842. The pub was demolished as part of the Queen's House development project undertaken by Ravenseft Properties in 1952. Following completion of Phase Three of this magnificent shopping and business complex it re-opened in 1955 and was re-licensed as The Bass House in February 1980.

Bass plc's origins date from 1777 when William Bass, an established carrier, bought a house in the renowned brewing town of Burton upon Trent and commenced brewing. The business flourished, his son, Michael Thomas Bass developing a thriving export business, shipping via Hull half of the company's production to the Baltic States and Hull playing an obvious major part in the company's early development. Bass took John Ratcliff into partnership in 1796 and John Gretton in 1835. Many company takeovers and mergers have followed since this time including ownership of Charrington and Company (established 1738), Worthington and Company (established 1744) and Mitchell's and Butler (established 1898). Bass plc was formed in 1979 and is the UK's largest brewer, at its peak in 1991, owning almost 7,000 pubs. Today, following the Monopoly and Mergers Commission Report (Beer Orders) legislation of 1989 allowing fairer competition in the market place, Bass control approximately 4,500 public houses.

Chapel Street takes its name from the former Providence Chapel which stood nearby in the late 1700s.

Bitter:   Stones
Lager:   Carling Black Label, Tennent's Pilsner
Cider:   Autumn Gold, Dry Blackthorn
Other:   Bass Mild, Guinness
Jukebox
**N.B.**   Closed Sunday lunch

## DRAM SHOP — BASS

A grocer and tea dealer, Thomas Gelson, occupied this site c.1806 (he had previously traded in High Street). By the mid-1830s it was under the proprietorship of George and Richard Gelson, who had obtained a licence to sell wine and spirits. The shop was known as the Two Lions, so called from the carved representations of two lions which stood in its doorway. It was bought by Henry Wilson, an established wine and spirit merchant, in 1849, who was reputed to have renamed the shop, 'On the Boards', as a tribute to the many members of the theatrical profession

*Dram Shop*                                                                 *Adam Stewart*

who frequented the place. These included Mr W F Wallett, the Queen's Theatre jester, and the then popular Mr Sims Reeves. The Queen's Theatre, formerly the Royal Amphitheatre, situated in Paragon Street, closed in 1869. Wallett was extremely popular in his day, although I would imagine his brand of humour would now earn him a visit from the Race Relations Board. An extract from his autobiography recalls one of his 'jests' whilst touring America:

*'As soon as the audience had left the large tent, John Murray, a gentleman who played the banjo extremely well, would sing and play in the dressing-room, until a crowd of negroes, who are passionately fond of music, would assemble outside to listen. When they had thus been engaged for some time, a party of us would take some short stakes and a long rope and, going near the gate of the field, would drive down the stakes in a line at short distances, and then tie the rope to the stakes six or eight inches from the ground, the banjo engrossing their attention at all time. As soon as the signal was given that all was prepared three of the performers were enclosed in an enormous framework representing giants. In an instant the side of the canvas would be raised; when giants and giantesses, clubs in hand, rushed out among the affrighted darkies, who fled away with fleet feet, making the nearest way to the gate. They often amounted to two or three hundred. In the hasty retreat and dim light, not observing the low rope, the front rank would be tripped up, and the others rolling over them, would pile up a hecatomb of black humanity. Then the stuffed clubs of the giants made awful havoc amongst them, and the terrified mob cried out "Murder" and implored mercy, the greater number tremblingly believing the giants were realities.'*

A bust of W F Wallett is in the possession of Hull Museums.

Henry Wilson's wine and spirit merchant's business thrived, supplying the majority of hard liquor and wines to the people of Hull. The old shop was demolished and handsome new premises were built during the late 1870s which he named Savile House. He also had large bonded warehouses in Sylvester Street, Dock Street and Hull Custom House, maturing stocks of whisky alone amounting to some 120,000 gallons by 1890. Savile House to this day is still fondly called Wilson's Corner by many local residents.

Part of this wine and spirit emporium became known as the Dram Shop by 1955, although this was not officially recognised until 1974, following a major refurbishment programme by Bass. Previously, Savile House itself held the licence. The Dram Shop with its rare circular bar, which was once thought to be the longest in Hull had it been straight, is little changed from when it was Henry Wilson's general office. It has without doubt the finest ornate pub ceiling, executed in Italian style, within the Hull district.

George Street was so named in honour of George III. Savile House takes its title from Savile Street, named after Sir George Savile, MP for York. He was an original shareholder in the Hull Dock Company, formed in the 18th century; part of the scheme involved laying out new roads to service these docks.

Bitter:  Stones[cc], Bass[cc], Everards Tiger[cc](g), Marston's Pedigree[cc](g), Boddingtons[cc](g) **N.B.** All guest beers changed regularly
Lager:  Carling Black Label, Tennent's Pilsner, Beck's
Cider:  Dry Blackthorn, Autumn Gold
Other:  Bass Mild[cc], Guinness
Sandwiches are available throughout its opening hours, seven days a week
Darts, Dominoes, Cribbage

## RUGBY TAVERN — SAMUEL SMITH'S

This house began trading as the Ship Molly c.1820 and at that time stood at the side of Queen's Dock, eventually filled in to make way for Queen's Gardens. It took its name from an American vessel, the *Molly*, which was built in New England in 1759 and became part of Hull's whaling fleet, plying its trade 1775-1806 until capture by the French. Her most famous captain was Angus Sadler who sailed her 1796-1802 and was the all-time

*Rugby Tavern*                    *Adam Stewart*

record whale catcher whilst in command of another sailing ship, the *Aurora*. In 1804 he brought home the produce of no fewer than 44 whales.

There is a painting of the *Molly* in Hull's Town Docks Museum along with many more exhibits of the town's sea-faring past and it is well worth a visit.

The name was changed to the Rugby by its then landlord John (Jack) Townend in 1900, who, at the time was also captain of Hull FC and made 142 appearances for the club. Hull folk have always given fanatical support to its rugby clubs, the crests of which are displayed on its sign. Jack Townend was the grandfather of the present John Townend, MP for Bridlington and chairman of the off-licence chain, the House of Townend. It was acquired by Sam Smith's in 1984, by which time it was abandoned and in a dilapidated state. The brewery embarked on a major redevelopment scheme and the pub had to be put on stilts whilst the improvements were carried out. It was re-opened in 1986 and a Civic Award was given for the tasteful way these alterations had been made.

Bitter:   Museum Ale[cc], Sam Smith's Old Brewery[cc]
Lager:    Ayingerbräu, Ayingerbräu D, Pils
Cider:    Sam Smith's Reserve
Other:    Sam Smith's Dark Mild, Sam Smith's Extra Stout
Bar meals and sandwiches are available Monday — Saturday, 12.00 noon — 2.00pm
Jukebox, Darts, Dominoes, Sky TV
**N.B.** This house is closed all day Sunday


## MANCHESTER HOTEL — BASS

Originally called the Salisbury Hotel, it was built during the 1880s. It was undoubtedly named after Cecil Robert Arthur Talbot Gascoyne (1830-1903) third Marquis of Salisbury. He was Prime Minister of Great Britain 1885-1886, 1886-1892, 1895-1902. Its name was changed to the Manchester Hotel in 1887 after its proprietor, Mr Ratcliffe Manchester.

On 5 May 1888, William Frederick Cody, otherwise known as Buffalo Bill, the famous American cowboy and frontiersman, gave his last performance of the first English tour of his Wild West Show at Hull's football ground, then situated on Holderness Road. Thousands of people flocked to see this living legend who had helped negroes escape from cotton plantations, was a boy rider of the Pony Express, served in the Union Army, fought in the Indian Wars, was ambushed by bandits and shot at by mail thieves. He had made plans to stay at Hull's Royal Station Hotel but was turned away upon his arrival. No doubt his six-foot, deerskin-clad frame, complete with stetson, moccasins, leather belt with ammunition pouches, hunting knife and hatchet proved too much for the management! Ratcliffe Manchester came to the rescue and put him up at his hotel.

He went straight to bed, the *Hull Arrow* reports,

*'And, after having had a couple of hours snooze in it on Friday afternoon, though it was in one of the top storeys, he remarked joyously that it suited him down to the ground. The consequence of that expression caused Mr. Proprietor Manchester to vigorously shake hands with himself, and, in all probability to double the wages of all the hotel attendants.'*

Buffalo Bill was to make a return visit to Hull, ending his last tour of England at Hull's Fairground, 1 and 2 July 1904.

From the end of the 1920s until 1971 the hotel was trading as the New Manchester. The former Trogg Bar (now Lasers) with its subdued lighting and cave-like decor designed during the 1960s, became the 'in' place for the younger townsfolk of Hull, and the pub retains the Edwardian splendour of bygone days in its appropriately named Edwardian Bar.

A licensee during the 1970s was Dick Gemmel, a Hull RFC star, who played for Great Britain four times before being injured out of the game. I have no doubt Buffalo Bill would have felt quite at home here, had he been around, when a shotgun was discharged in this house on 15 May 1987.

*Manchester Hotel*                                                                 *Adam Stewart*

Bitter:    Bass<sup>cc</sup>, Stones<sup>cc</sup>
Lager:    Carling Black Label
Cider:    Autumn Gold, Dry Blackthorn
Other:    Bass Mild<sup>cc</sup>, Guinness
Bar meals and sandwiches are served Monday — Saturday, 12.00 noon — 2.00pm
Dartboard, Dominoes, Sky TV
**N.B.**    Closed Sunday lunch.


## THE INSTITUTE — LEYLAND HOUSE

The Institute, a Grade II listed building, was built for James Alderson who named this magnificent residence Albion House. It is difficult to say how long he was resident here as the Hull directories show him living at his father's home, variously described as No. 4 and 15 Charlotte Street, between 1840 and 1842. The only reference I have been able to find of him located at this address is contained within the 1846 directory, by which time he had left Hull. James Alderson was honorary physician at the Royal Infirmary from 1829-1845. The hospital, which stood where the Prospect Centre is now, was demolished in 1972. He resigned his position on 5 September 1845 and returned to London where he had previously practised and went on to become President of the Royal College of Physicians and a Fellow of the Royal Society. He was knighted in November 1869 and became Physician Extraordinary to Queen Victoria in 1874. There is a bust of James Alderson in Hull's Town Docks Museum, an odd place you may think to display this eminent doctor, but he was the first man to dissect a whale.

His father, Dr John Alderson, preceded James as honorary physician at the Infirmary from 1792-1829 and was held in high esteem by the townsfolk of Hull: he was a public benefactor when he offered to vaccinate the poor, free of charge, against an epidemic of smallpox which was rife in 1802. His statue now stands in front of Hull's present Royal Infirmary, opened by HM the Queen on 16 June 1967. When he died in September 1829 it was estimated that 12-15,000 mourners attended his funeral.

To return to Albion House, after James Alderson's departure, Dr Robert Fewster Horner took up residence. He was also a physician at Hull Royal Infirmary and had applied to fill the position left vacant upon John Alderson's death, but withdrew on learning that James, John's son, was applying. Although they disagreed on many medical matters, they must have remained firm friends, for Dr Horner paid generous tribute to John Alderson at his farewell luncheon.

The Church of England Religious and Literary Society, formed in 1855, originally met in Osborne Street, their objective being to advance

The Institute
*Jonathan White*

the principles of the Church of England and to promote the study of literature and science amongst its members. It changed its name to the Hull Church Institute in 1858, acquired Albion House, re-arranging the accommodation to include a news room, library, chess, draughts and whist rooms. The opening ceremony on 16 November 1865 was presided over by the Lord Mayor, Alderman H J Atkinson, and was attended by a 'Who's Who' of Hull's leading Victorian citizens. The *Eastern Morning News* reported:

*'The company began to arrive at half-past six and in a short time the rooms became thronged with a fashionable assemblage. So crowded, indeed, that it might have been supposed some noble Lord was holding a reception in the middle of the season, and that he had issued, as customary, invitations to about thrice the number of people his mansion was capable of accommodating.'*

The building was damaged during the Blitz but in more recent years part was used by Hull Subscription Library. A property development company from Leeds, ADP International, was granted a licence to develop the Institute into a pub and it started serving ale for the first time in January 1991. ADP subsequently went into receivership and the pub is currently controlled by another Leeds development company, Leyland House, which took over on 31 October 1992.

The Institute is said to have a poltergeist. Managers past and present have been at a loss to explain how objects have been mysteriously moved. The present incumbent has even gone to the trouble of having the house blessed by the Rev. Tom Willis of Bridlington in July 1992. The clergyman, one of the York Diocese's 'ghostbusters', told me that the ceremony was particularly difficult and much holy water was used and many crosses laid during the exorcism.

Albion Street was named after a famous warship of the day. *The Albion*, built in Hull and launched in 1763, fought at the battles of Grenada and Martinique and was wrecked in 1797. A model of *The Albion* is contained within Trinity House.

Bitter:   John Smith's[cc], Directors[cc], Webster's[cc]
Lager:   Miller Pilsner, Foster's, Kronenbourg, Carlsberg Export, Carlton LA
Cider:   Dry Blackthorn, Autumn Gold
Other:   Wilson's Mild, Beamish
Bar meals and sandwiches are available Monday, 11.30am — 3.00pm, Tuesday — Saturday, 11.30am — 7.30pm
Darts, Dominoes, Chess and Draughts

## THE SHIRE HORSE — JOSHUA TETLEY

The Broadway opened on this site for Moor and Robson brewers in June 1933. The opening ceremony was presided over by the Lord Mayor, Alderman J M Dosser: previously the site was occupied by the Grapes Hotel c.1820. It was closed in March 1973 by its then owners, Bass Limited, because fire regulations could not be met; at that time it was also a residential hotel.

It re-opened again to the delight of real ale buffs as Hull's first free house, trading under the name of the Grob and Ducat in 1977. This pub in turn was closed down on Boxing Day 1979 having been sold to Joshua Tetley. The lovers of real ale went into deep mourning. The brewery re-opened it on 17 January 1980 as The Shire Horse. Shire Horses were once a common sight in the fields of rural England and the name brings back memories of the Clydesdales used by Hull Brewery Company. These magnificent equines were once employed by the brewery to pull their dreys and rullies. Several were retained throughout the 1960s and 70s as show horses. They never failed to draw a crowd, bedecked in their full regalia of highly polished leather harness with brass trappings on show days. Today the pub has become a mecca for Hull's more youthful drinkers following the new vogue of drinking imported beers from the bottle, much, I dare say, to the chagrin of its former CAMRA followers.

Ferensway was named in honour of Hull's best-known philanthropist, Thomas Robinson Ferens (1847-1930). From modest beginnings he rose to become chairman of one of Hull's greatest companies, Reckitt's (now Reckitt and Coleman plc) and Liberal MP for East Hull (1906-1918). In later years he used his wealth to the lasting benefit of the people of Hull, giving the site and a large endowment to establish Hull University, creating the Ferens Art Gallery, and being heavily involved, along with Sir James Reckitt, in the formation in East Hull of the Garden Village.

Bitter:   Tetley[cc]
Lager:   Castlemaine XXXX, Skol, Löwenbräu
Cider:   Olde English, Copperhead
Other:   Guinness
Bar meals and sandwiches are available Monday — Saturday 12.00 noon — 2.00pm
Dartboard, Satellite TV
**N.B.** This house is closed Sunday lunchtime.

*The Shire Horse*                                             *Adam Stewart*

*Monroe's*

Adam Stewart

## MONROE'S — JOSHUA TETLEY

This public house stands on or very near the site of the oddly named Jack on a Cruise, c.1800. A former Gleadow and Dibb house, it stood on what was a highly populated tenement area, North Street. It was certainly trading some 130 years later until the Hull Brewery Company had it rebuilt as the Spencers Arms in 1931 during the layout of Ferensway. Although the street takes its name from a different source, the brewery named this house in honour of George John Spencer, 2nd Earl of Sunderland, a distinguished former First Lord of the Admiralty.

It was rebuilt yet again in 1956, at a cost of £78,000. For a short time during the 1980s North Country Breweries, then the owners, called it Shenanigans. This name proved to be unpopular with the locals, and it promptly reverted to its old name. It was sold to the Brent Walker Group, headed by the flamboyant George Walker. His brother, former British boxing champion, Billy Walker, was guest of honour in September 1989 at the re-opening ceremony after it had been totally re-themed and renamed Monroe's. An unusual feature of this pub is the life-size model of Marilyn Monroe at its entrance in a scene from the film *The Seven Year Itch*. Marilyn was born Norma Jean Baker in 1926 and became one of Hollywood's greatest stars, her screen credits including *The Asphalt*

61

*Jungle* and *The Misfits*. She undoubtedly was, in her prime, the world's greatest sex symbol, her *'little girl next door'* innocence, blonde hair and shapely figure making her the envy of almost every woman in the western world and the dream of every man.

Marilyn was found dead, lying naked in her bed on 5 August 1962, reputedly dying of an overdose of Nembutal sleeping tablets. She was to became the first in a trio of tragedies. Her suicide has never been universally accepted. She had previously enjoyed extremely close relationships with the then President of the United States, John Fitzgerald Kennedy, and his brother, Attorney-General Robert Kennedy, and it was thought by some that she was *'silenced'* after threatening to go public over these affairs. John was assassinated on 22 November 1963 and Robert was shot dead on 5 June 1968. This house is full of pictures and posters depicting Marilyn's life. The Brent Walker Group were put into receivership and the pub was sold to Joshua Tetley in May 1992.

Spencer Street is named after a Dr Spencer of York who had owned a public house here in the 19th century.

Bitter: Tetley
Lager: Castlemaine XXXX, Skol, Löwenbräu
Cider: Copperhead, Olde English
Other: Guinness
Bar meals and sandwiches are available Monday — Saturday, 12.00 noon — 2.00pm
Sky TV
**N.B.**This house is closed all day Sunday

# FOOTNOTE

You will notice along your travels that not every public house within the confines of these tours is mentioned, as it would be impracticable to include them all. They are nonetheless still worth a visit and will be the subject of another *Bottoms Up*. Of those which are mentioned, beers on offer are listed at the time of writing, including guest beers, but it is worth remembering that breweries and landlords are apt to change them quite frequently. I have tried to include as wide a variety of brews as possible but it is clear that both Mansfield and Bass are dominant within the City.

This guide is in no way a critical look at the public houses mentioned, for I believe every house has features to commend it. As for the quality of ale you must make up your own mind. The historical background is not intended to provide a comprehensive history, only selected information from source material which is often limited. For any errors or omissions I take full responsibility.

Drinking, of course, should be a pleasurable experience, so, should you embark upon any one of these tours, remember to pace yourself. For those of you thinking of organising a pub crawl for charity, you will need to obtain written permission from the police station responsible for the area you will be drinking in. It would also be a good idea to inform the publicans in advance of your plans.

For obvious reasons you will find these tours all the more enjoyable midweek and I am sure that all the landlords, from a business point of view, would agree with this.

Happy Drinking!